The Collector's Guide to

Post Cards

Jane Wood

L.-W. Promotions
P.O. Box 69
Gas City, Indiana

Additional copies of this book may be ordered from:

L.-W. Promotions
P.O. Box 69
Gas City, Indiana 46933

@ $9.95 Add $2.00 for postage and handling.

Values Updated 1993

1 2 3 4 5 6 7 8 9 0

Printed by IMAGE GRAPHICS, Paducah, Kentucky

TABLE OF CONTENTS

ACKNOWLEDGEMENTS

The beautiful color section was provided by Catherine Durbin, 120 West North "A" Street, Gas City, Indiana 46933. Catherine is an advanced collector and is interested in buying rare and special interest cards. Catherine is retired and spends much of her time traveling the Midwest buying and showing at Postcard Shows & Sales. Many thanks to her.

Others who contributed greatly were:

Russell Russ, Marion IN
George Luckeydoo, Newark OH
Howard Johnson, Marion IN
Jim Roush, Marion IN
John Murray, Hinsdale IL
Wayne Reedy, Middletown IN
Rex Lyons, Swayzee IN
Sally Carver, Brookline MA.

A special thanks to Forrest Lyons and Robert Stoker of Marion, Indiana. Robert is a serious collector of cards and was the photographer for most of the artist section. Forrest is the author of two books on Postcards, (now out of print) from which some of the pages in this book appeared.

INTRODUCTION

This book is intended only as a reference book for values of cards and as a guide to different types of cards available for collectors. No small book could completely cover postcard collecting, but we have tried to show the work of many different artists, some publishers and other collectible categories.

For easy reference, all cards are priced below the row in which they appear, reading from top to bottom. All cards in the book are priced to be in excellent condition. Cards in mint condition would naturally bring more, while cards in lower grades of condition would bring less.

The values of cards in this book are intended as a guide only. Regional differences and areas of high collector interest would naturally cause great price fluctuations especially in the view card area.

HALLOWEEN

1. $7.00-8.00
2. $7.00-8.00
3. $7.00-8.00
4. $7.00-8.00
5. $7.00-8.00
6. $7.00-8.00

1. $7.00-8.00
2. $7.00-8.00
3. $7.00-8.00
4. $7.00-8.00

1. $7.00-8.00
2. $7.00-8.00
3. $7.00-8.00
4. $7.00-8.00

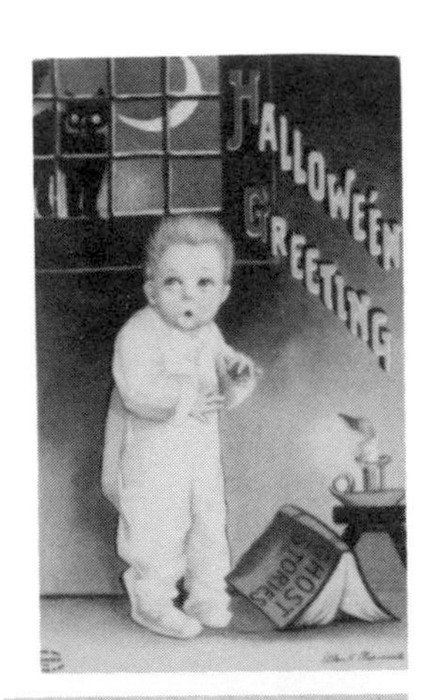

1. $7.00-8.00*
2. $5.00-8.00
3. $7.00-8.00
4. $50.00-60.00**

*Clapsaddle
**Winsch

1. $1.00-1.50
2. $1.00-2.00
3. $1.00-2.00
4. $15.00-17.50
5. $1.00-1.50
6. $15.00-17.50

1. $ .25 - .50
2. $5.00-6.00
3. $ .25 - .50
4. $2.00-3.00

1. $2.00-2.50
2. $1.00-1.50
3. $1.00-2.00
4. $2.00-2.50

1. $1.00-2.00
2. $1.00-2.00
3. $3.50-4.50
4. $3.00-3.50

SANTA CLAUS

1. $1.00-2.00
2. $3.00-4.00
3. $9.00-11.00
4. $10.00-12.00
5. $3.00-4.00
6. $9.00-11.00

1. $7.00-9.00
2. $5.00-6.00
3. $5.00-6.00
4. $2.00-3.00

1. $7.00-8.00
2. $3.00-4.00
3. $5.00-6.00
4. $7.00-8.00

1. $2.00-3.00
2. $7.00-8.00
3. $7.00-8.00
4. $2.00-3.00

1. $1.00-2.00
2. $3.00-4.00
3. $ .50-1.00
4. $1.00-2.00
5. $1.00-2.00
6. $3.00-4.00

1. $1.00-2.00
2. $ .50-1.00
3. $1.00-2.00
4. $ .50-1.00
5. $1.00-2.00
6. $ .50- .75

1. $1.00-2.00
2. $2.00-3.00
3. $1.00-2.00
4. $4.00-5.00

1. $4.00-5.00
2. $ .50-1.00
3. $ .25- .50
4. $ .25- .50

EASTER

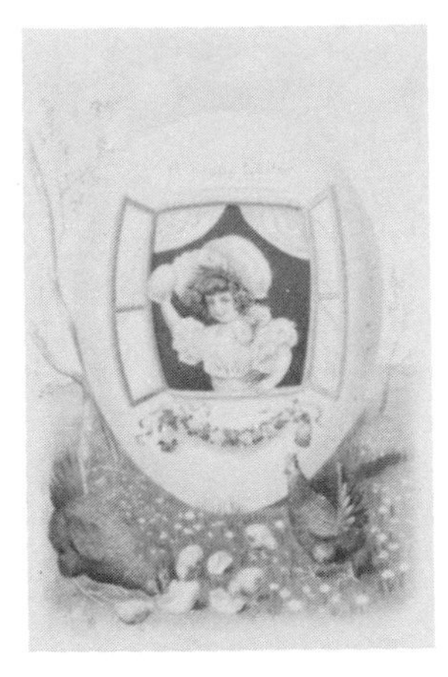

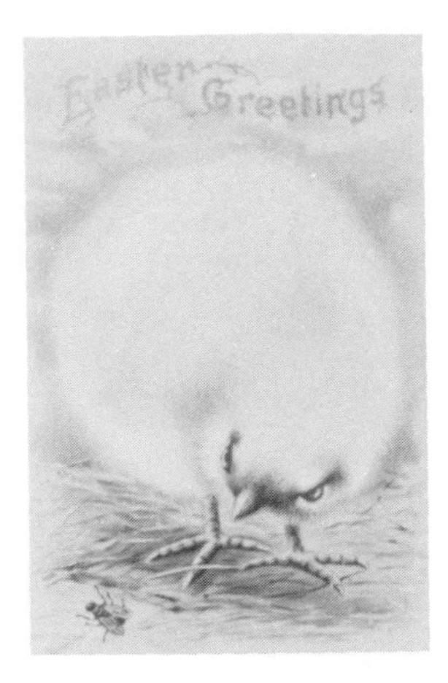

1. $2.00-3.00
2. $3.00-4.00
3. $5.00-6.00 **
4. $1.00-2.00
5. $2.00-3.00
6. $2.00-3.00

1. $1.00-2.00
2. $ .50- .75
3. $3.00-4.00
4. $20.00-22.50

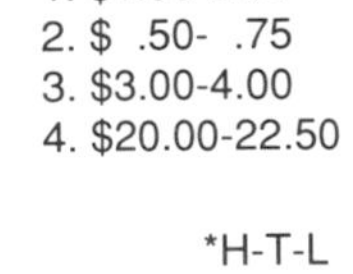

1. $ .50-1.00
2. $3.00-4.00
3. $1.00-2.00
4. $ .50-1.00

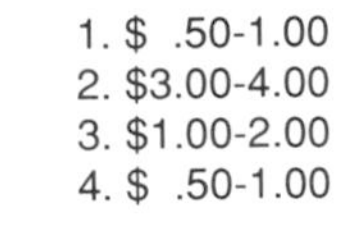

1.$ .50-1.00
2.$ 3.00-4.00
3. $3.00-4.00
4. $ .50 - .75

*H-T-L
**Winsch

1. $4.00-5.00
2. $4.00-5.00
3. $6.00-7.00
4. $4.00-5.00

1. $4.00-5.00
2. $4.00-5.00
3. $4.00-5.00
4. $4.00-5.00

1. $3.00-4.00
2. $5.00-6.00
3. $4.00-5.00
4. $4.00-5.00

1. $5.00-6.00
2. $4.00-5.00
3. $4.00-5.00
4. $6.00-7.00

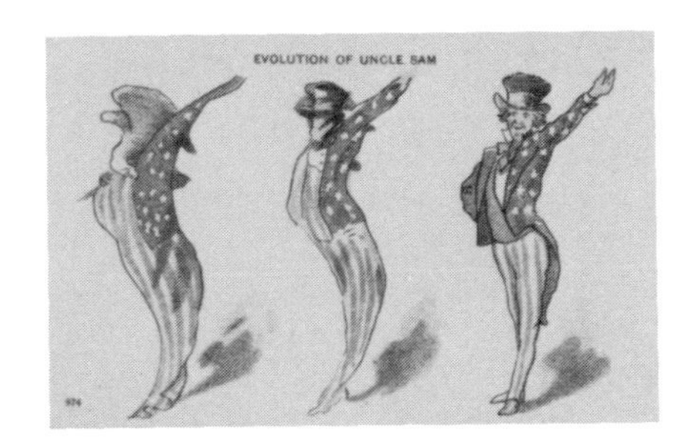

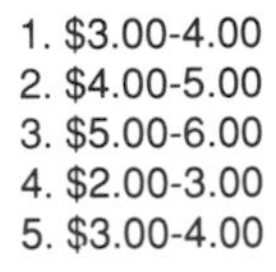
1. $3.00-4.00
2. $4.00-5.00
3. $5.00-6.00
4. $2.00-3.00
5. $3.00-4.00

1. $4.00-5.00
2. $2.00-3.00
3. $2.00-3.00

1. $3.00-4.00
2. $4.00-5.00
3. $4.00-5.00
4. $4.00-5.00
5. $4.00-5.00

1. $2.00-3.00
2. $1.00-2.00
3. $1.00-2.00
4. $ .25- .50
5. $3.00-4.00
6. $3.00-4.00

1. $ .50 - .75
2. $1.00 - 1.50
3. $2.00-3.00
4. $2.00-3.00

1. $4.00-5.00
2. $2.00-3.00
3. $10.00-12.00
4. $ .50 - .75

1. $2.00-3.00
2. $1.00-2.00
3. $2.00-3.00
4. $2.00-3.00

ST. PATRICK'S DAY

1. $1.00-2.00
2. $1.00-2.00
3. $2.00-3.00
4. $2.00-3.00
5. $1.00-2.00
6. $1.00-2.00

1. $1.00-2.00
2. $1.00-2.00
3. $1.00-2.00
4. $1.00-2.00
5. $1.00-2.00
6. $1.00-2.00

1. $1.00-2.00
2. $2.00-3.00
3. $1.00-2.00
4. $4.00-5.00

1. $3.00-4.00
2. $3.00-4.00
3. $3.00-4.00
4. $4.00-5.00

Elevated R. R. and Station, Delaware Avenue, Philadelphia, Pa.

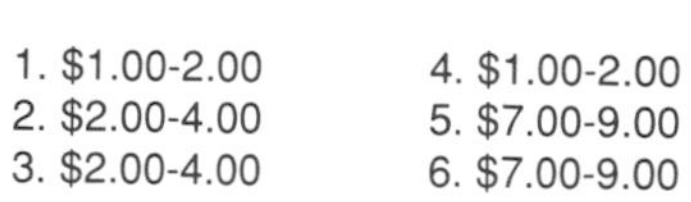

General Electric Co. Erie, Pa.
Gas Electric Motor Car
Largest Electric Locomotive in the World

1. $1.00-2.00
2. $2.00-4.00
3. $2.00-4.00
4. $1.00-2.00
5. $7.00-9.00
6. $7.00-9.00

1. $1.00-3.00
2. $ .50-1.00
3. $2.00-3.00
4. $1.00-1.50
5. $1.00-1.50
6. $10.00-12.00

1. $ .50-1.00
2. $ .50-1.00
3. $ .50-1.00
4. $ .50-1.00

1. $ .50-1.00
2. $ .50-1.00
3. $ .50-1.00
4. $ .50-1.00

TRAINS & DEPOTS

All cards $2.00-6.00

Union Depot and Park, Ogden, Utah.
On Line of Union Pacific.

15. BIG FOUR DEPOT AND DEEP CUT, WABASH, IND.

Loading Sherman Gravel near Buford, Wyo.
On Line of Union Pacific.

All cards $3.50-5.50

Cameron House and C. M. & St. P. Passenger Station, La Crosse, Wis.

All cards $4.00-5.50

All cards $ .50-1.00 except bottom right card, $3.00-4.00.

CHURCHES

All cards $ .50-1.00

All cards $10.00-15.00

STATE CAPITOLS

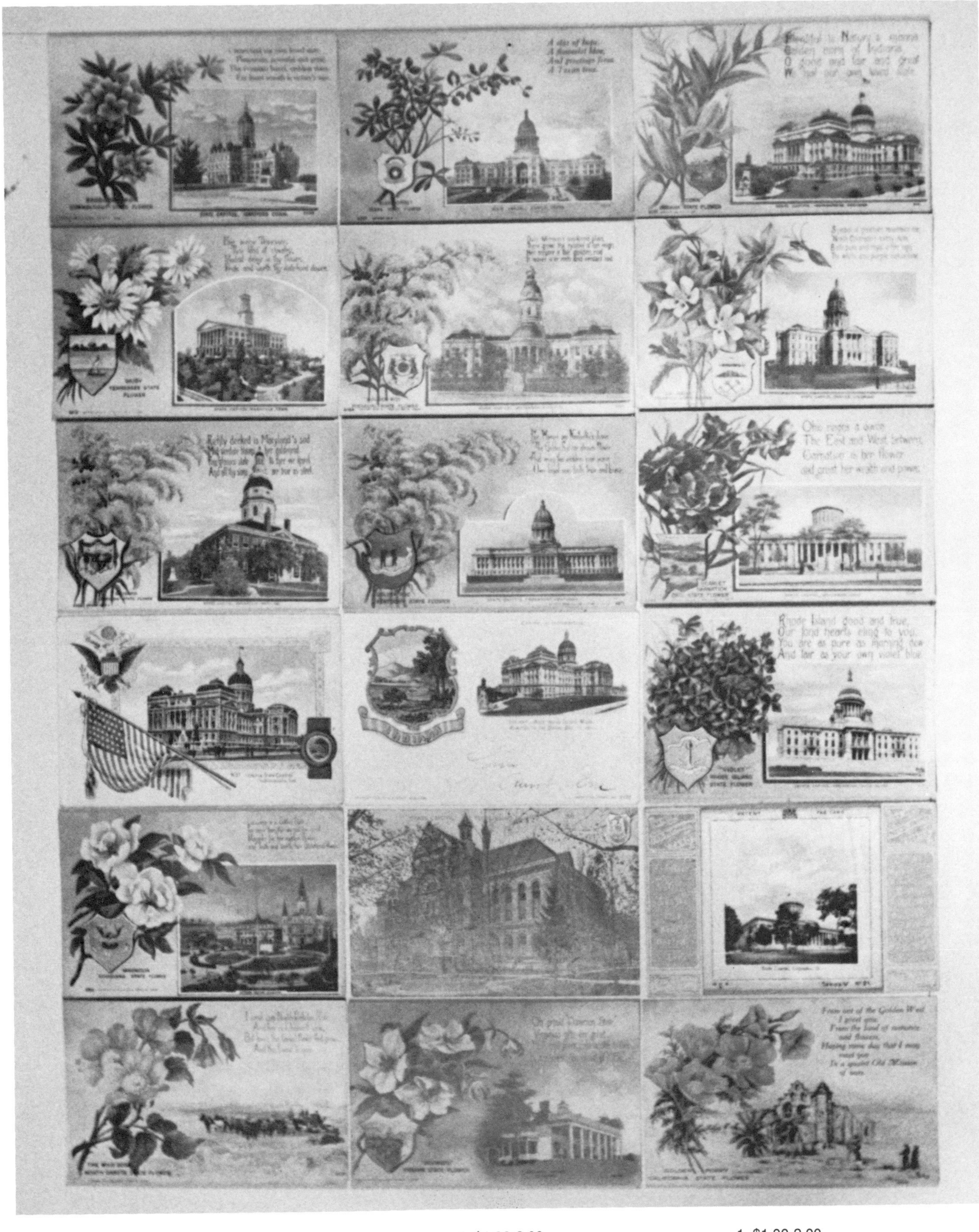

1. $1.00-2.00
2. $1.00-2.00
3. $1.00-2.00
4. $4.00-5.00
5. $1.00-2.00
6. $1.00-2.00

1. $1.00-2.00
2. $1.00-2.00
3. $1.00-2.00
4. $1.00-2.00
5. $2.00-3.00
6. $1.00-2.00

1. $1.00-2.00
2. $1.00-2.00
3. $1.00-2.00
4. $1.00-2.00
5. $10.00-12.00
6. $1.00-2.00

All cards $1.00-2.00

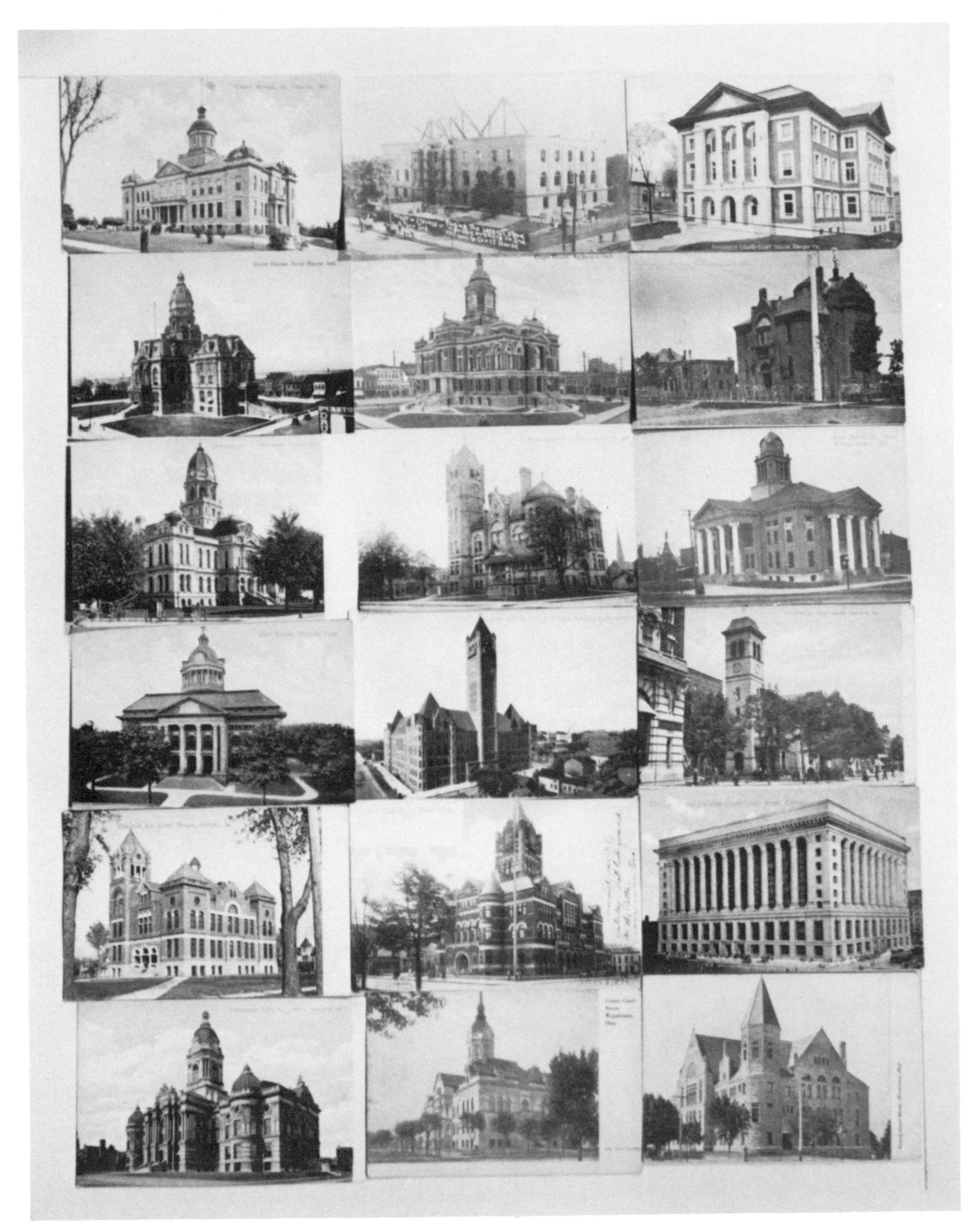

All cards $2.50-3.50

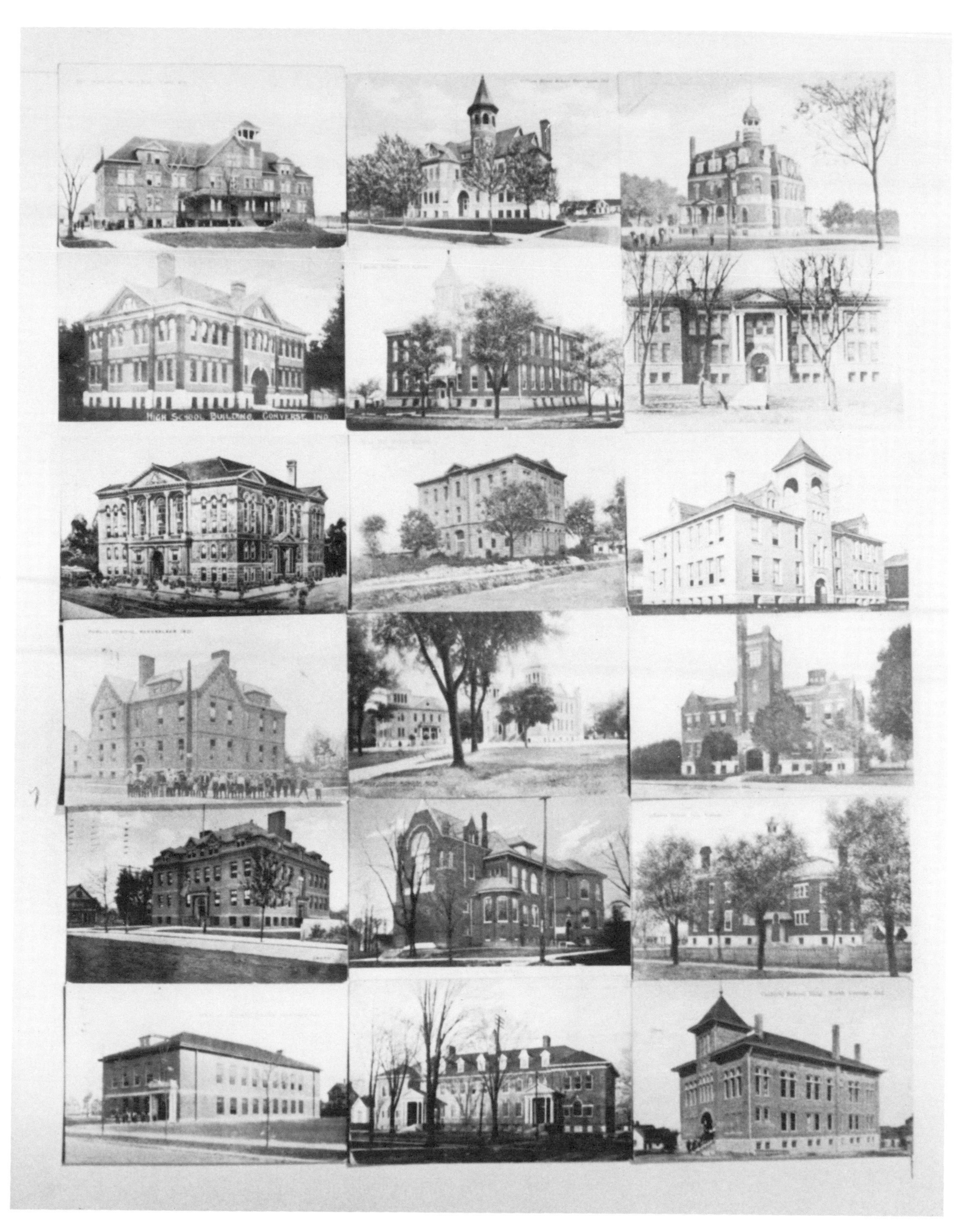

All cards $2.00-2.50

All cards $1.50-2.50

All cards $3.50-5.00

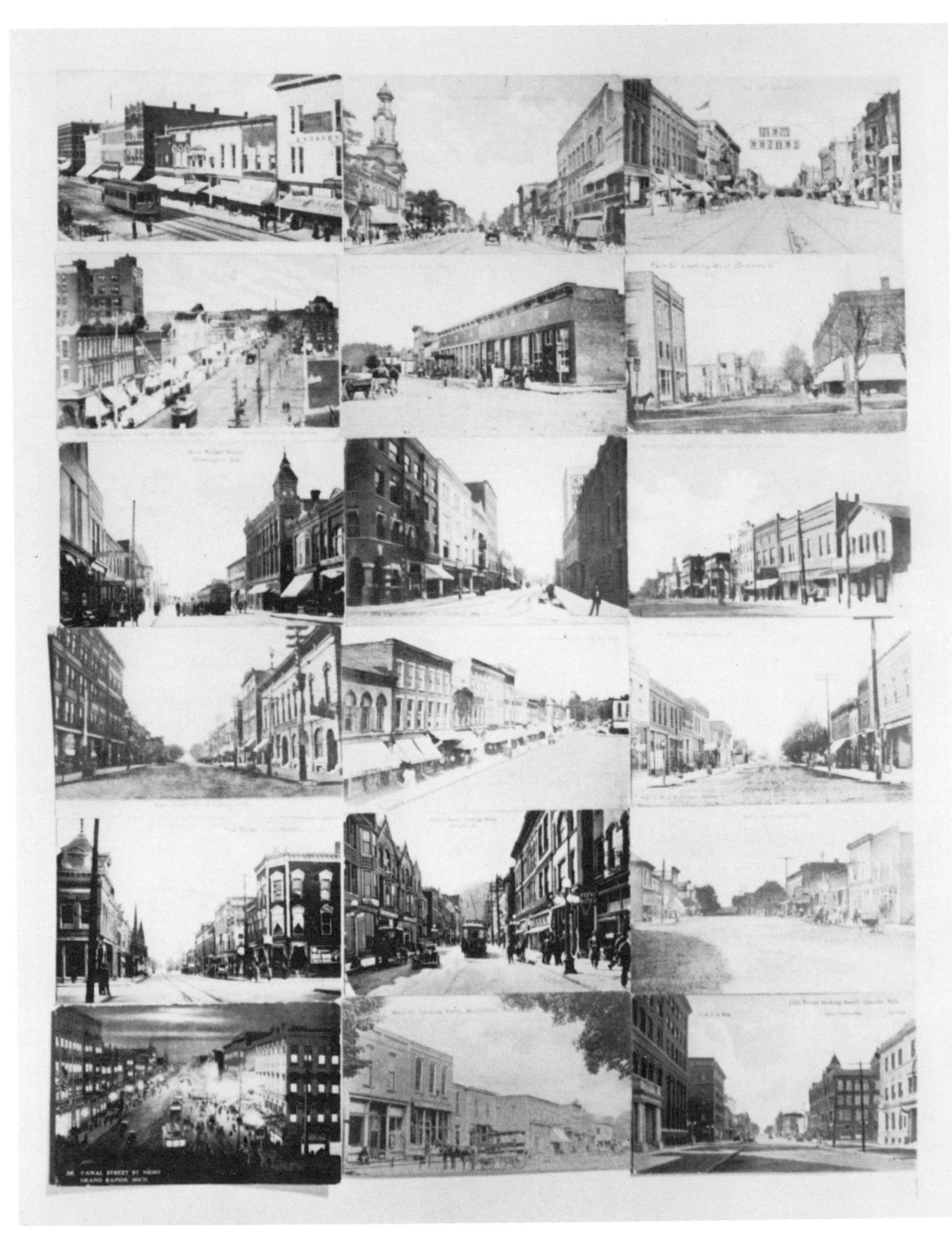

All cards $3.50-5.00

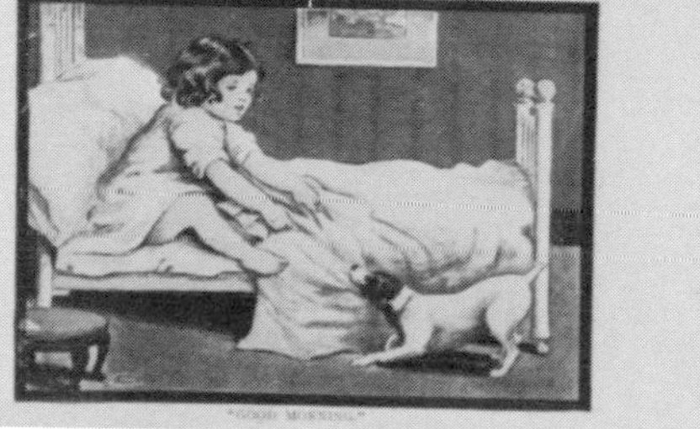

1. $2.00-3.00
2. $3.00-4.00
3. $4.00-5.00
4. $1.00-2.00
5. $4.00-5.00*

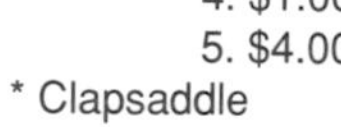

* Clapsaddle

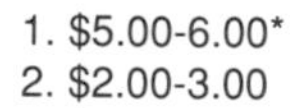

1. $5.00-6.00*
2. $2.00-3.00
3. $5.00-6.00*
4. $1.00-2.00

1. $6.00-7.00*
2. $4.00-5.00
3. $2.00-3.00
4. $3.00-4.00

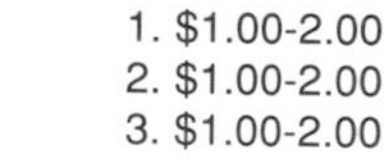

1. $1.00-2.00
2. $1.00-2.00
3. $1.00-2.00

CHILDREN

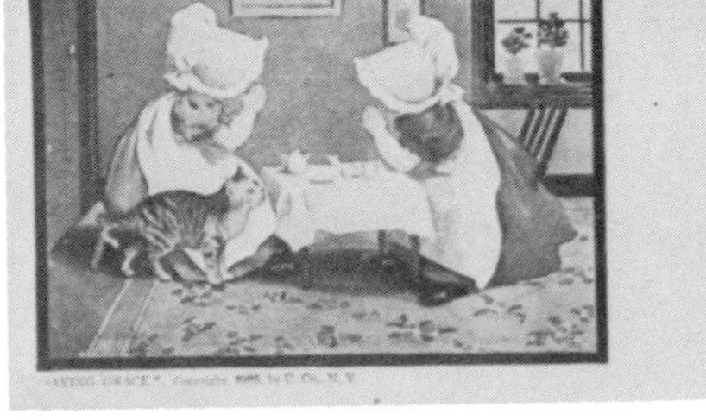

1. $2.00-3.00
2. $3.00-4.00
3. $2.00-3.00
4. $3.00-5.00
5. $2.00-3.00*

1. $1.00-2.00
2. $6.00-8.00*
3. $7.00-9.00*

1. $1.00-2.00
2. $1.00-1.50
3. $6.00-7.00*

1. $3.00-4.00
2. $4.00-5.00
3. $2.00-3.00

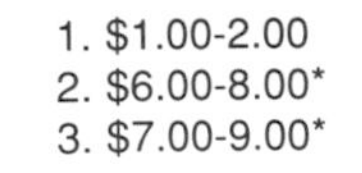

1. $7.00-9.00

2. $7.00-9.00

* Silk

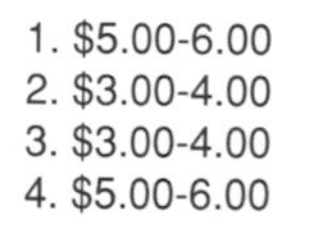
1. $5.00-6.00
2. $3.00-4.00
3. $3.00-4.00
4. $5.00-6.00

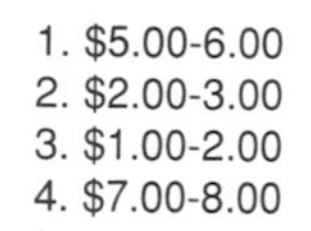
1. $5.00-6.00
2. $2.00-3.00
3. $1.00-2.00
4. $7.00-8.00

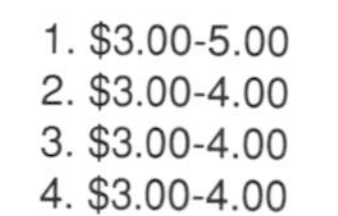
1. $3.00-5.00
2. $3.00-4.00
3. $3.00-4.00
4. $3.00-4.00

1. $5.00-6.00
2. $2.00-3.00
3. $2.00-3.00
4. $4.00-5.00

FOLLIES & SILK DRESSES

1. $2.00-3.00
2. $2.00-3.00
3. $2.00-3.00
4. $2.00-3.00

*Silk

1. $5.00-6.00
2. $5.00-6.00
3. $5.00-6.00
4. $5.00-6.00

1. $5.00-6.00
2. $5.00-6.00
3. $5.00-6.00
4. $15.00-20.00

1. $8.00-10.00*
2. $8.00-10.00*
3. $8.00-10.00*
4. $8.00-10.00*

1. $6.00-8.00*
2. $4.00-6.00*
3. $8.00-10.00*
4. $8.00-10.00*

1. $25.00-35.00
2. $25.00-27.00
3. $25.00-35.00
4. $25.00-35.00
5. $25.00-35.00
6. $25.00-35.00

1. $25.00-35.00
2. $20.00-25.00
3. $25.00-35.00
4. $25.00-35.00
5. $25.00-35.00
6. $20.00-25.00

1. $25.00-35.00
2. $25.00-35.00
3. $25.00-35.00
4. $25.00-35.00
5. $18.00-20.00
6. $75.00-100.00

HOLD-TO-LIGHT

1. $15.00-20.00
2. $30.00-40.00
3. $30.00-40.00

1. $25.00-35.00
2. $125.00-135.00
3. $35.00-45.00

1. $30.00-40.00
2. $35.00-40.00
3. $25.00-35.00

1. $125.00-135.00
2. $10.00-15.00
3. $12.00-15.00

1. $12.00-15.00
2. $4.00-6.00
3. $12.00-15.00
4. $4.00-6.00

1. $8.00-10.00
2. $10.00-12.50
3. $5.00-8.00
4. $5.00-7.00

1. $12.00-15.00
2. $30.00-35.00*
3. $30.00-35.00*
4. $30.00-35.00*

1. $30.00-35.00*
2. $12.00-15.00
3. $30.00-35.00*
4. $30.00-35.00*

*Silk **Clapsaddle

1. $5.00-7.00
2. $5.00-7.00
3. $5.00-7.00
4. $5.00-7.00

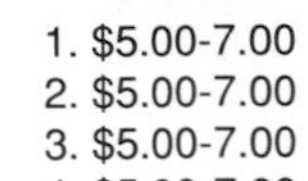

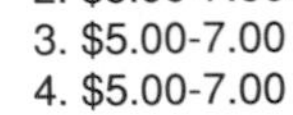

1. $5.00-7.00
2. $5.00-7.00
3. $5.00-7.00
4. $5.00-7.00

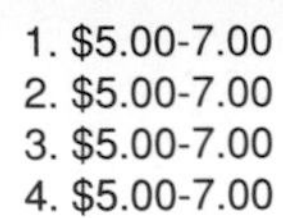

1. $5.00-7.00
2. $5.00-7.00
3. $5.00-7.00
4. $5.00-7.00

1. $5.00-7.00
2. $5.00-7.00
3. $5.00-7.00
4. $50.00-60.00*

*Mechanical

1. $7.00-9.00
2. $4.00-6.00
3. $10.00-12.50
4. $10.00-12.00

1. $10.00-12.00
2. $4.00-6.00
3. $10.00-12.50
4. $25.00-35.00

1. $4.00-6.00
2. $15.00-20.00
3. $15.00-20.00
4. $15.00-20.00

1. $10.00-12.00
2. $25.00-35.00
3. $25.00-35.00

4. $10.00-12.00
5. $5.00-7.00*

*Celluloid

CATS

1. $3.00-4.00
2. $1.00-2.00
3. $10.00-12.00
4. $3.00-4.00

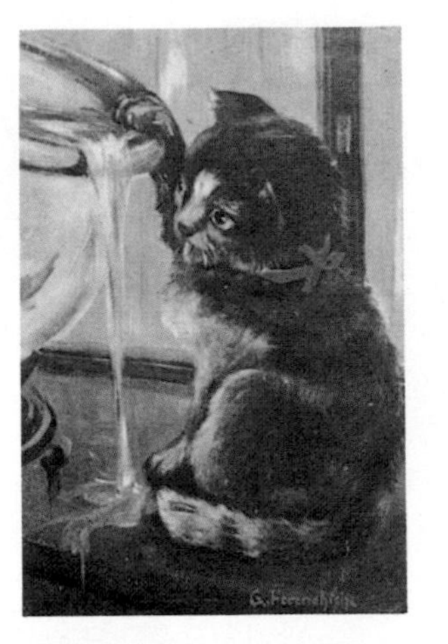

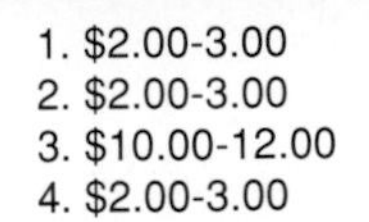
1. $2.00-3.00
2. $2.00-3.00
3. $10.00-12.00
4. $2.00-3.00

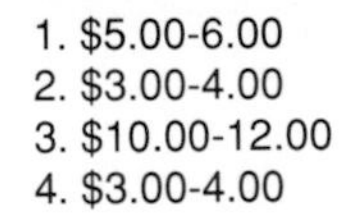
1. $5.00-6.00
2. $3.00-4.00
3. $10.00-12.00
4. $3.00-4.00

1. $7.00-8.00
2. $1.00-2.00
3. $3.00-4.00
4. $3.00-4.00
5. $2.00-3.00
6. $2.00-3.00

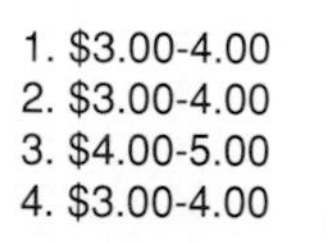
1. $3.00-4.00
2. $3.00-4.00
3. $4.00-5.00
4. $3.00-4.00

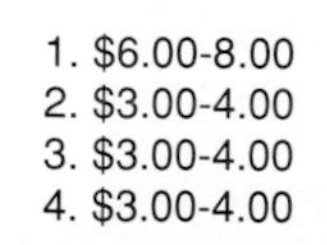
1. $6.00-8.00
2. $3.00-4.00
3. $3.00-4.00
4. $3.00-4.00

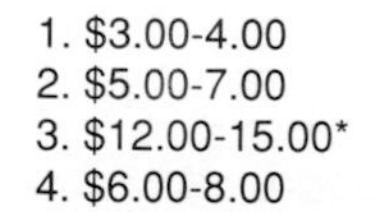
1. $3.00-4.00
2. $5.00-7.00
3. $12.00-15.00*
4. $6.00-8.00

1. $3.00-4.00
2. $3.00-4.00
3. $3.00-4.00
4. $6.00-8.00
5. $3.00-4.00
6. $6.00-8.00

*Brundage

CLAPSADDLE

1. $4.00-5.00
2. $10.00-12.50
3. $6.00-7.50
4. $8.00-10.00

1. $6.00-7.50
2. $6.00-8.00
3. $10.00-12.50
4. $10.00-12.50

1. $8.00-10.00
2. $6.00-7.50
3. $10.00-12.50
4. $12.00-15.00

1. $5.00-7.00
2. $6.00-8.00
3. $5.00-6.00
4. $3.00-4.00

1. $15.00-20.00
2. $10.00-12.00
3. $1.00-2.00
4. $1.00-2.00
5. $55.00-60.00
6. $55.00-60.00

1. $6.00-8.00
2. $13.00-15.00
3. $11.00-13.00
4. $17.00-20.00

1. $15.00-20.00
2. $12.00-15.00
3. $11.00-13.00
4. $55.00-60.00

1. $15.00-20.00
2. $12.00-15.00
3. $15.00-17.00
4. $55.00-60.00

FANTASY

1. $17.00-20.00
2. $3.00-5.00
3. $5.00-7.00
4. $4.00-6.00

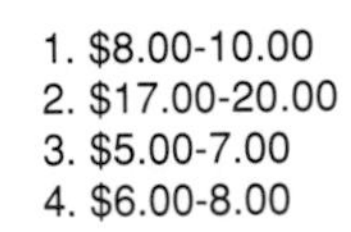

1. $8.00-10.00
2. $17.00-20.00
3. $5.00-7.00
4. $6.00-8.00

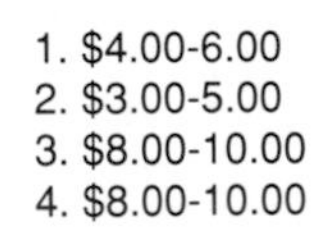

1. $4.00-6.00
2. $3.00-5.00
3. $8.00-10.00
4. $8.00-10.00

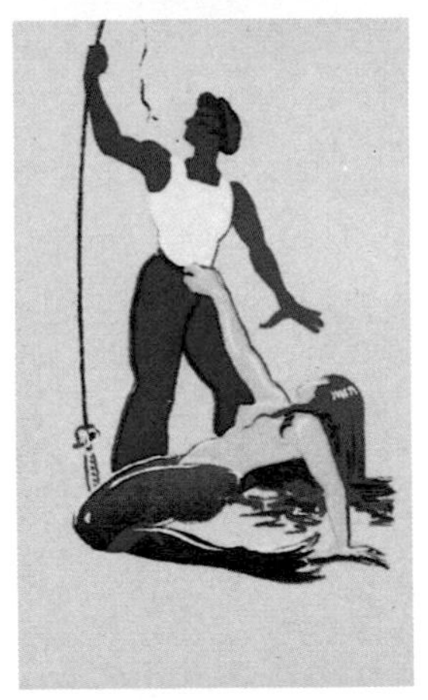

1. $6.00-8.00
2. $12.00-15.00
3. $17.00-20.00
4. $3.00-5.00

1. $2.00-3.00
2. $4.00-6.00
3. $6.00-8.00
4. $4.00-5.00

1. $3.00-4.00
2. $8.00-10.00
3. $6.00-8.00
4. $4.00-5.00

1. $2.00-3.00
2. $3.00-4.00
3. $5.00-7.00
4. $4.00-5.00

1. $4.00-6.00
2. $6.00-8.00
3. $5.00-7.00
4. $4.00-6.00

ART CARDS

1. $5.00-7.00
2. $3.00-4.00
3. $3.00-4.00
4. $10.00-12.00

1. $5.00-7.00
2. $8.00-12.00
3. $3.00-4.00
4. $40.00-45.00*

1. $5.00-7.00
2. $20.00-30.00
3. $3.00-4.00
4. $3.00-4.00

1. $35.00-40.00
2. $35.00-40.00
3. $15.00-17.00
4. $40.00-45.00*

*Winsch

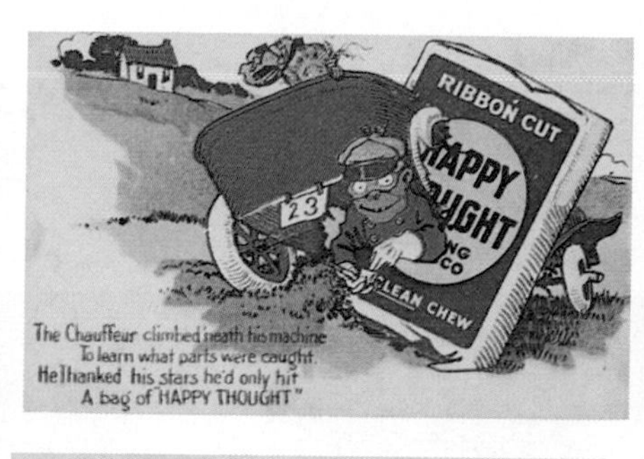

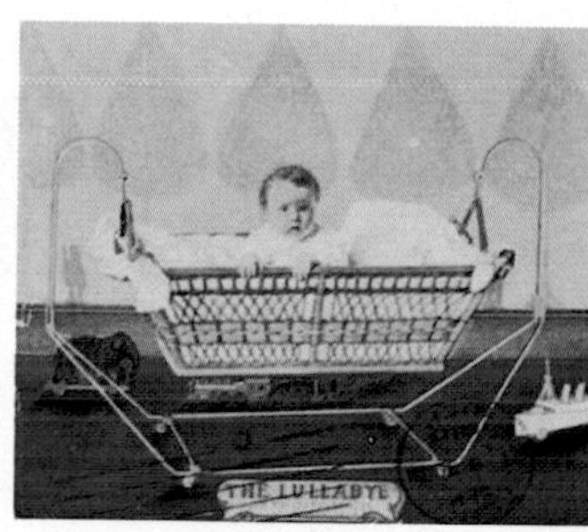

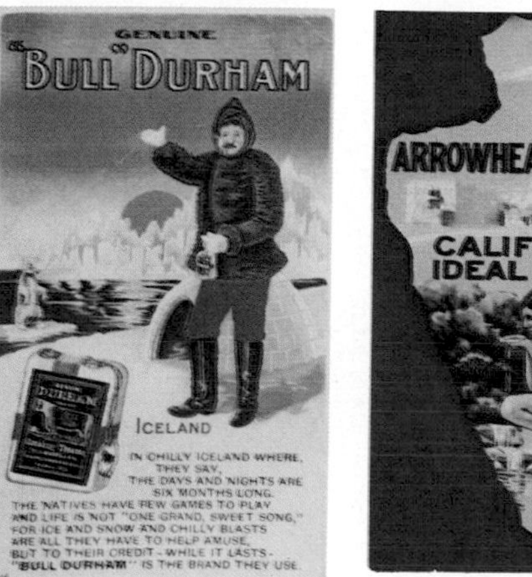

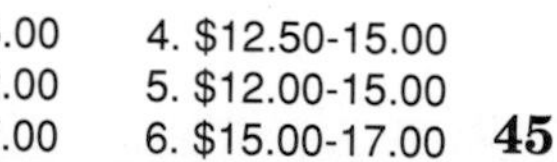

1. $12.00-15.00
2. $15.00-20.00
3. $15.00-16.00
4. $15.00-20.00

1. $12.00-15.00
2. $15.00-20.00
3. $6.00-8.00
4. $10.00-12.00

1. $6.00-7.00
2. $12.00-15.00
3. $12.00-15.00
4. $6.00-8.00
5. $25.00-27.00
6. $18.00-20.00

1. $12.00-15.00
2. $10.00-12.00
3. $15.00-17.00
4. $12.50-15.00
5. $12.00-15.00
6. $15.00-17.00

TUCK PRESIDENTS

All cards $8.00-10.00

SOUVENIR FROM
DALLAS, TEX.

There is always plenty to do here.

1. $15.00-20.00
2. $35.00-37.00
3. $35.00-37.00
4. $12.00-15.00

WE WANT YOUR RECORD ORDERS
Every record in stock
VICTOR and COLUMBIA
See Sharp
THE ROBT. D. SHARP MUSIC COMPANY
823-825 15th Street
DENVER, COLO.
Look for the sign "ALL THINGS MUSICAL"

"NO, MA'AM, I AINT SEEN NO
STRAY ROOSTER OVER HEAH."

1. $25.00-27.00*
2. $25.00-30.00
3. $30.00-40.00
4. $20.00-25.00

*Homemade O' Neill

Groeten uit s' Gravenhage

I WAS SURPRISED TO HEAR FROM YOU!

DIRECTIONS—
Move Lever From Side to Side.

1. $4.00-6.00
2. $12.00-15.00
3. $4.00-6.00
4. $30.00-35.00

Not a lemon in this garden of love, but a peach.

A joyful
Easter.
Greeting.

A MERRY
CHRISTMAS

1. $7.00-9.00
2. $8.00-10.00
3. $15.00-20.00
4. $30.00-35.00

MISC. POSTCARDS

1. $20.00-22.00
2. $6.00-8.00
3. $6.00-8.00
4. $3.00-5.00

1. $5.00-7.00
2. $4.00-6.00
3. $4.00-6.00
4. $35.00-40.00**

*P.F.B.
**O' Neill

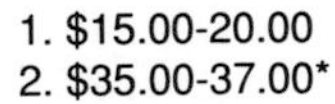

1. $15.00-20.00
2. $35.00-37.00*
3. $7.00-9.00
4. $4.00-6.00

1. $5.00-7.00
2. $3.00-5.00
3. $10.00-12.50
4. $10.00-12.00

1. $2.00-3.00
2. $3.00-5.00
3. $3.00-5.00
4. $2.00-3.00
5. $1.00-2.00
6. $5.00-6.00

1. $2.00-3.00
2. $5.00-6.00
3. $7.00-8.00
4. $5.00-6.00

1. $2.00-3.00
2. $3.00-4.00
3. $2.00-3.00
4. $3.00-4.00
5. $10.00-12.00
6. $2.00-3.00

LARGE CARDS

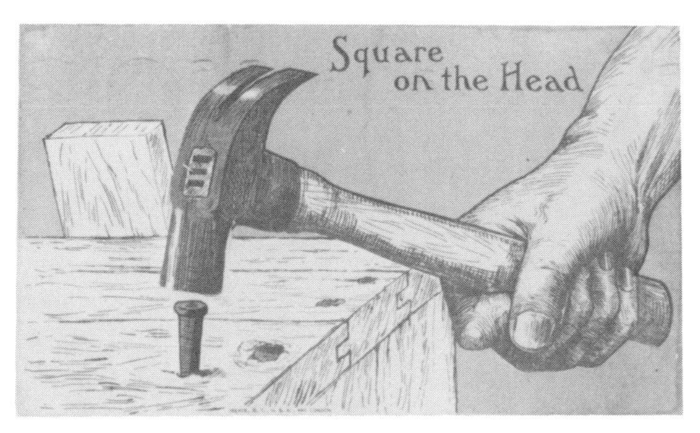

All cards $20.00-30.00

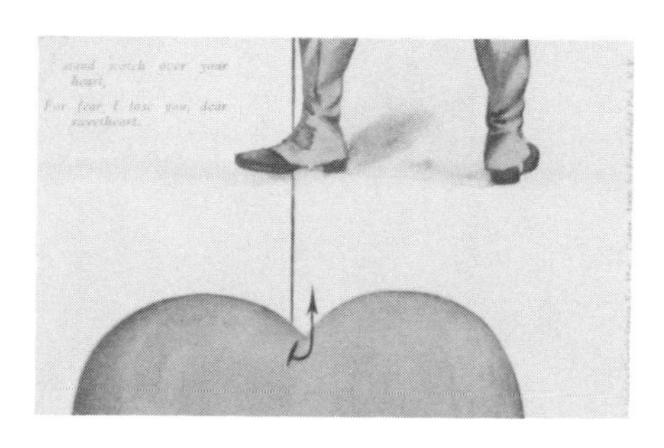

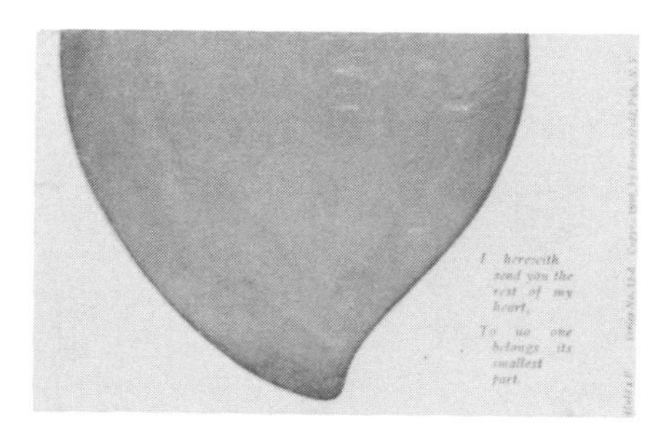

Fisherman $60.00 set

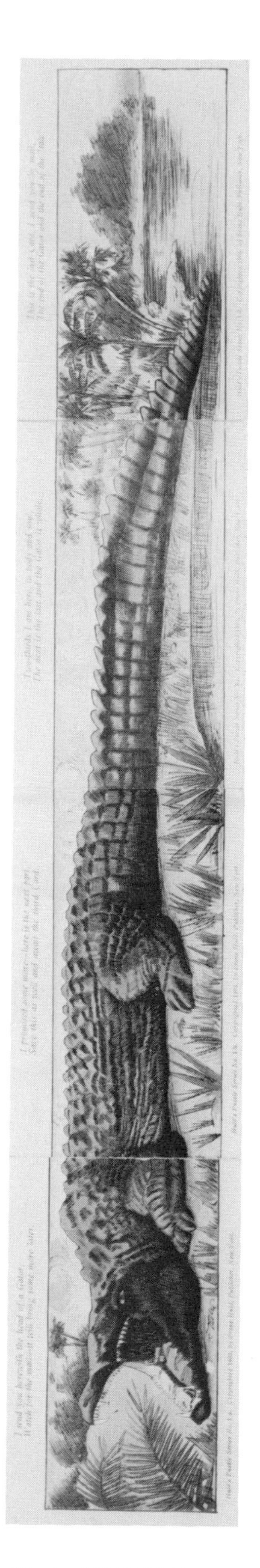

Alligator $22.50-30.00

Uncle Sam $80.00-100.00 set
Santa Claus $90.00-100.00
The fish story $20.00-25.00 set

1. $4.00-5.00
2. $5.00-6.00
3. $4.00-5.00
4. $4.00-5.00

1. $1.00-2.00
2. $1.00-2.00
3. $3.00-4.00
4. $5.00-6.00
5. $3.00-4.00
6. $3.00-4.00

1. $5.00-6.00
2. $4.00-5.00
3. $ .50-1.00
4. $4.00-6.00
5. $1.00-2.00
6. $7.00-10.00

1. $10.00-12.50
2. $2.00-3.00
3. $10.00-12.50
4. $10.00-12.50

EXPOSITION – JAMESTOWN

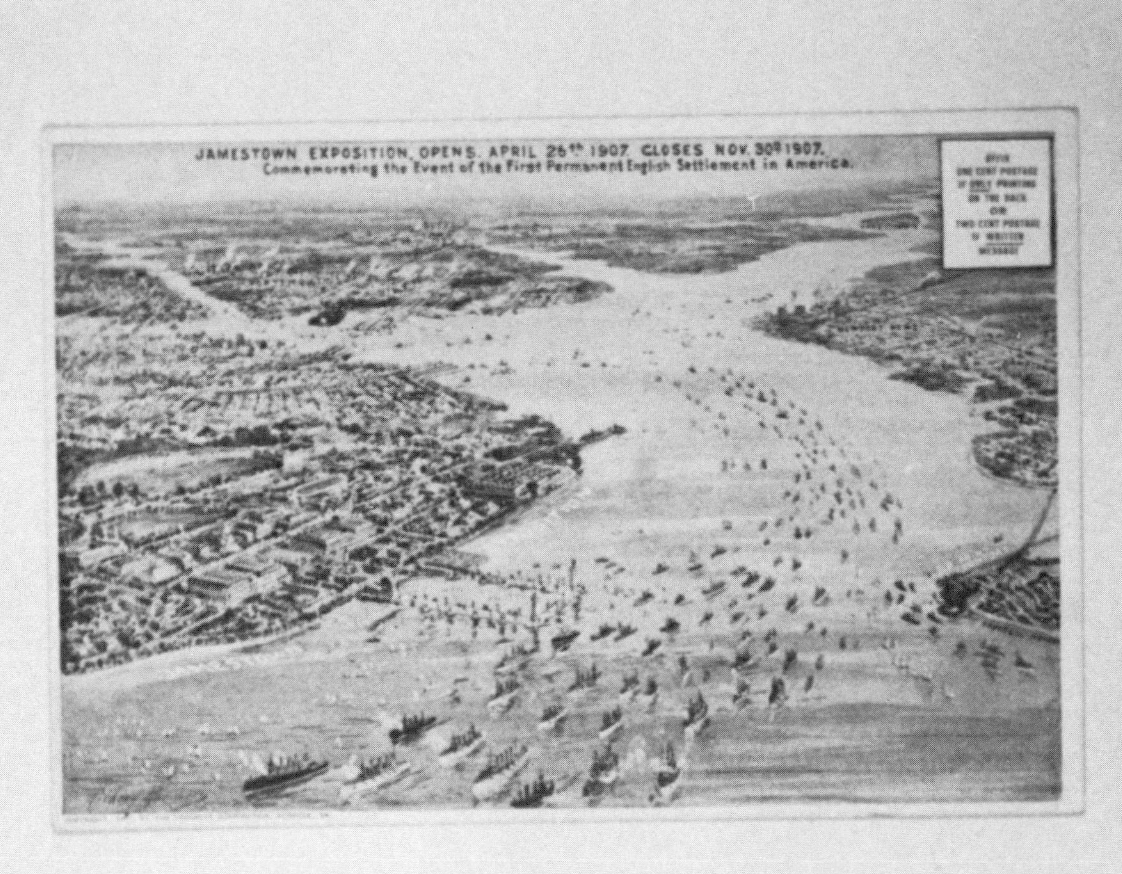

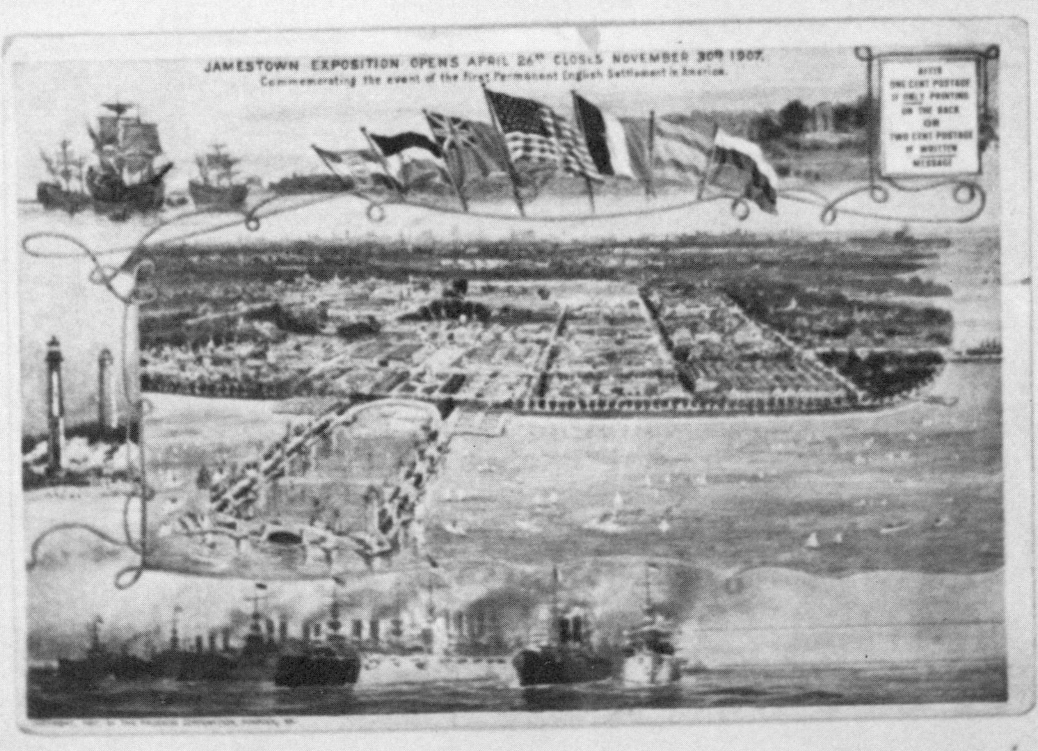

All Cards $50.00-75.00

All cards $4.00-5.00 except last vertical row $10.00-15.00

CHARLES A. LINDBERGH

All cards $12.50-15.00

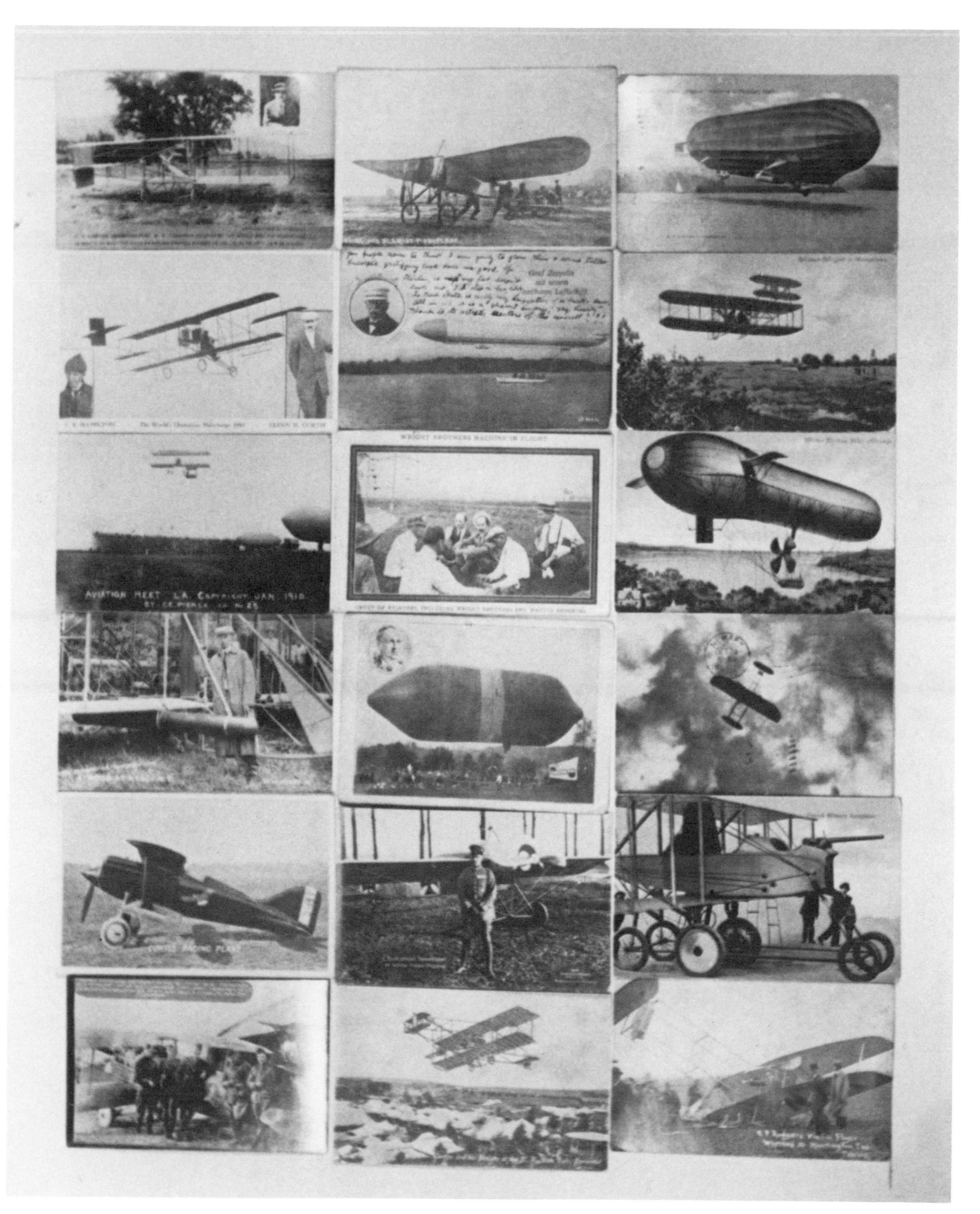

All cards $15.00-20.00

1. $17.50-20.00
2. $10.00-12.00
3. $15.00-17.50
4. $6.00-8.00
5. $15.00-17.50

1. $15.00-17.50
2. $1.00-2.00
3. $6.00-8.00
4. $2.00-3.00
5. $2.00-3.00

1. $2.00-3.00
2. $2.00-3.00
3. $7.00-9.00
4. $15.00-17.50
5. $15.00-17.50

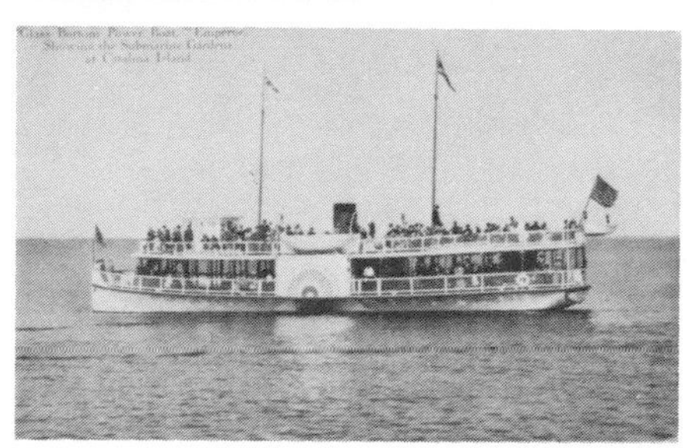

1. $2.00-3.00
2. $2.00-2.50
3. $2.00-2.50
4. $2.00-3.00
5. $2.00-3.00
6. $2.00-3.00

1. $2.00-3.00
2. $2.00-3.00
3. $2.00-3.00
4. $2.00-3.00
5. $2.00-3.00
6. $2.00-3.00

1. $4.00-5.00
2. $2.00-3.00
3. $2.00-3.00
4. $3.00-4.00
5. $4.00-5.00
6. $2.00-3.00

1. $7.00-10.00
2. $10.00-15.00
3. $25.00-30.00
4. $3.00-4.00
5. $20.00-25.00
6. $12.50-15.00

1. $3.00-4.00
2. $3.00-4.00
3. $3.00-4.00
4. $2.00-3.00
5. $10.00-15.00
6. $2.00-3.00

1. $2.00-3.00
2. $3.00-5.00
3. $5.00-7.00
4. $10.00-15.00
5. $10.00-15.00

All cards $2.00-3.00

MILITARY

1. $1.00-2.00
2. $2.00-3.00
3. $2.00-3.00
4. $2.00-3.00
5. $2.00-3.00

1. $2.00-3.00
2. $2.00-3.00
3. $4.00-5.00
4. $2.00-3.00
5. $2.00-3.00

1. $4.00-5.00
2. $2.00-3.00
3. $1.00-2.00
4. $1.00-2.00

1. $2.00-3.00	1. $2.00-3.00	1. $2.00-3.00
2. $2.00-3.00	2. $2.00-3.00	2. $2.00-3.00
3. $2.00-3.00	3. $2.00-3.00	3. $2.00-3.00
4. $5.00-7.50*	4. $2.00-3.00	4. $2.00-3.00
5. $2.00-3.00	5. $2.00-3.00	5. $2.00-3.00
6. $2.00-3.00	6. $2.00-3.00	6. $2.00-3.00

*Russle

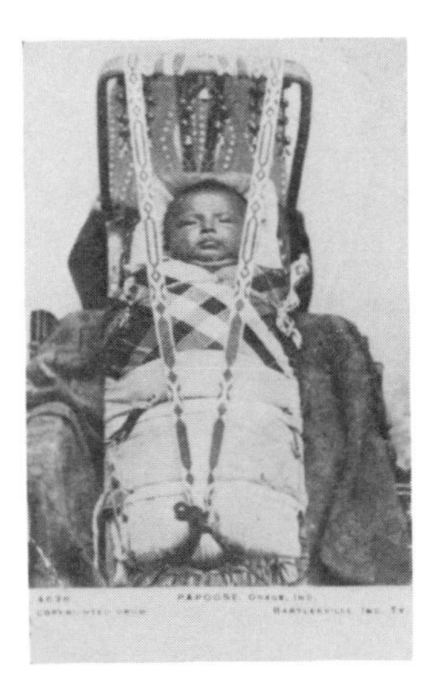

1. $4.00-5.00
2. $3.00-4.00

1. $3.00-4.00
2. $3.00-4.00

1. $1.00-2.00
2. $3.00-4.00

1. $3.00-4.00
2. $3.00-4.00

1. $4.00-5.00

2. $2.00-3.00

3. $5.00-6.00

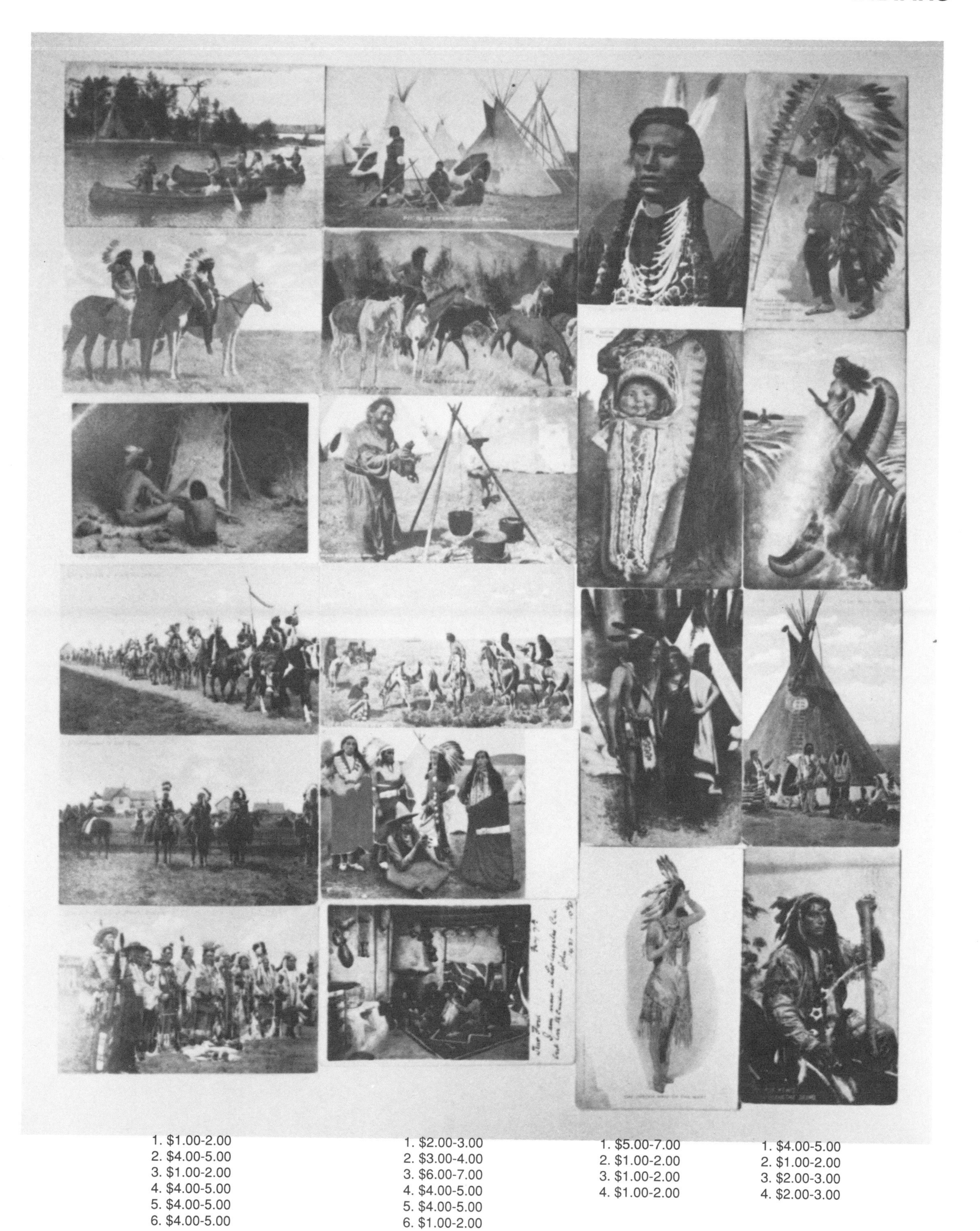

1. $1.00-2.00
2. $4.00-5.00
3. $1.00-2.00
4. $4.00-5.00
5. $4.00-5.00
6. $4.00-5.00

1. $2.00-3.00
2. $3.00-4.00
3. $6.00-7.00
4. $4.00-5.00
5. $4.00-5.00
6. $1.00-2.00

1. $5.00-7.00
2. $1.00-2.00
3. $1.00-2.00
4. $1.00-2.00

1. $4.00-5.00
2. $1.00-2.00
3. $2.00-3.00
4. $2.00-3.00

All cards $5.00-6.00
Embossed & Colorful

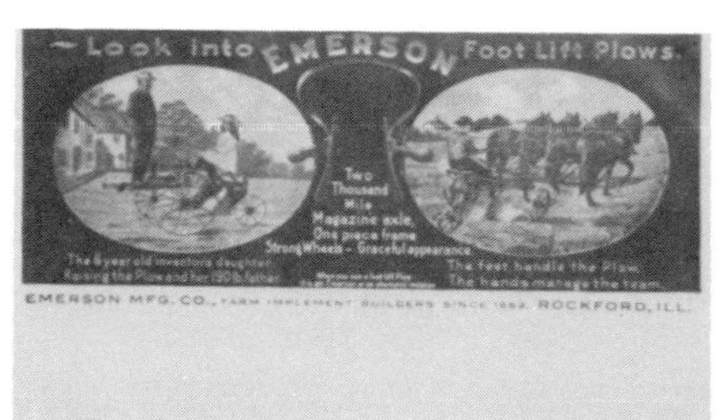

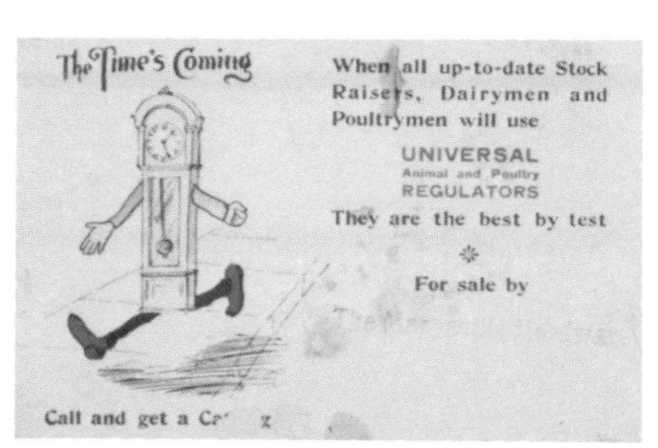

1. $12.00-15.00
2. $12.00-15.00
3. $5.00-7.00
4. $3.00-4.00
5. $10.00-12.50
6. $4.00-5.00

1. $6.00-7.00
2. $6.00-7.00
3. $4.00-5.00
4. $4.00-5.00
5. $15.00-20.00
6. $4.00-5.00

1. $7.50-10.00
2. $5.00-6.00
3. $10.00-12.50
4. $6.00-10.00

1. $10.00-12.50
2. $8.00-9.00
3. $12.50-15.00
4. $5.00-6.00

1. $12.00-15.00
2. $5.00-7.50
3. $10.00-12.50
4. $10.00-12.50

1. $15.00-17.50
2. $6.00-7.50
3. $2.00-3.00
4. $7.00-8.50

1. $17.50-22.50
2. $8.00-10.00
3. $10.00-12.50
4. $10.00-12.50
5. $8.00-10.00
6. $ 1.00-2.50

1. $20.00-25.00
2. $3.00-4.00
3. $3.00-4.00
4. $3.00-4.00
5. $3.00-4.00
6. $7.00-10.00
7. $5.00-7.50

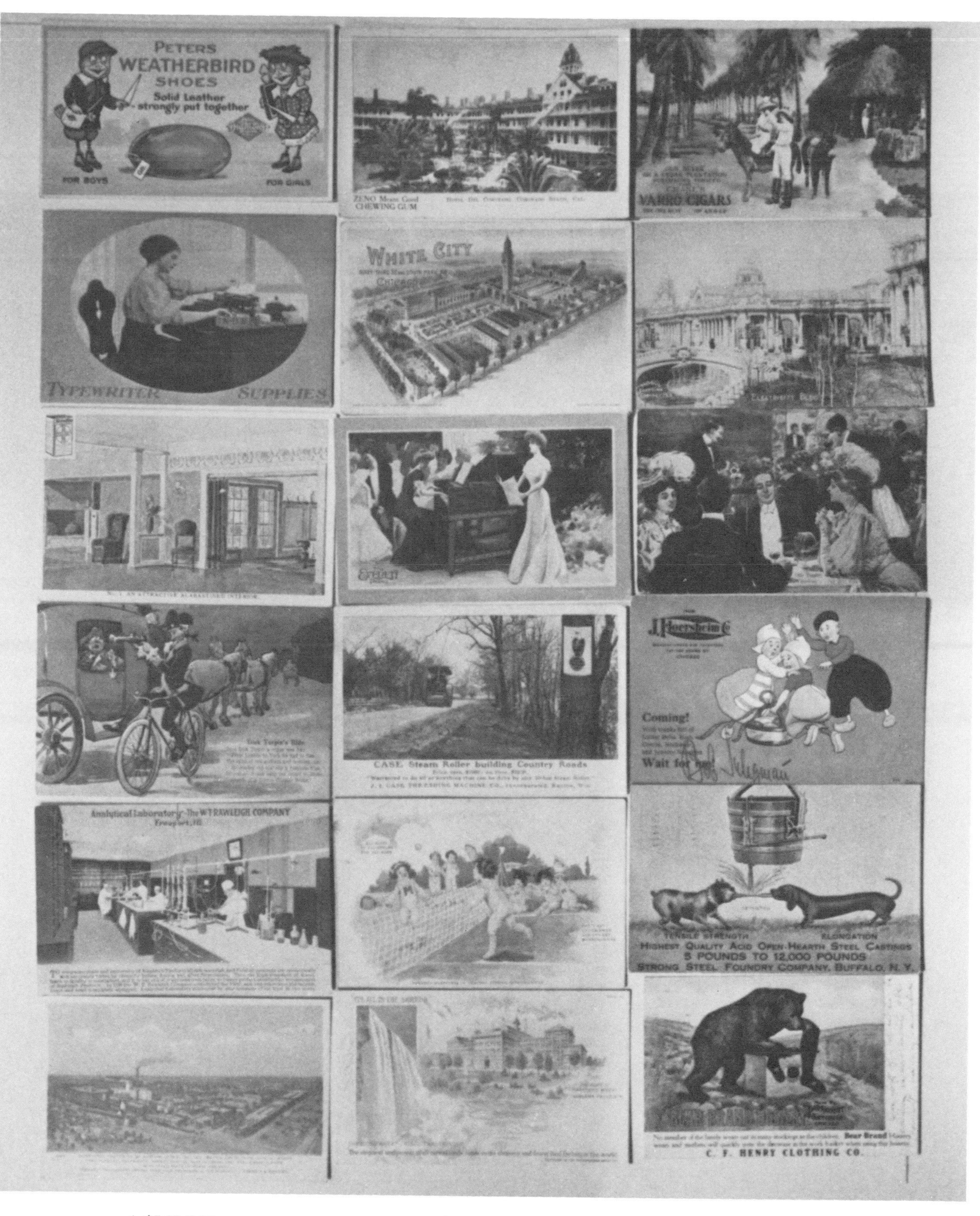

1. $5.00-7.50
2. $10.00-15.00
3. $5.00-6.00
4. $7.00-10.00
5. $6.00-7.50
6. $3.00-5.00

1. $3.00-5.00
2. $3.00-4.00
3. $5.00-6.00
4. $2.00-3.00
5. $10.00-12.50
6. $1.00-2.00

1. $5.00-7.00
2. $2.00-3.00
3. $5.00-7.00
4. $6.00-8.00
5. $10.00-15.00
6. $4.00-5.00

1. $20.00-22.50
2. $20.00-22.50
3. $20.00-22.50
4. $20.00-25.00
5. $20.00-22.50
6. $10.00-15.00

1. $20.00-22.50
2. $20.00-22.50
3. $20.00-22.50
4. $20.00-22.50
5. $20.00-22.50
6. $20.00-22.50

1. $20.00-22.50
2. $20.00-22.50
3. $20.00-22.50
4. $20.00-22.50
5. $20.00-22.50
6. $6.00-7.00

Dogs $30.00-35.00
Birds & Animals $40.00-45.00

1. $25.00-30.00
2. $20.00-25.00
3. $20.00-25.00
4. $20.00-25.00

1. $7.00-8.00
2. $4.00-5.00
3. $7.00-10.00
4. $7.00-10.00
5. $25.00-30.00
6. $25.00-30.00

1. $25.00-30.00
2. $30.00-35.00
3. $30.00-35.00
4. $5.00-7.00
5. $30.00-35.00
6. $7.00-10.00

1. $15.00-17.50
2. $12.00-17.50
3. $30.00-35.00
4. $30.00-35.00

1. $30.00-35.00
2. $30.00-35.00
3. $30.00-35.00

1. $10.00-12.50
2. $10.00-12.50
3. $10.00-12.50
4. $10.00-12.50
5. $10.00-12.50
6. $25.00-30.00

1. $4.00-5.00
2. $4.00-5.00
3. $4.00-5.00
4. $4.00-5.00
5. $4.00-5.00
6. $4.00-5.00

1. $10.00-12.50
2. $10.00-12.50
3. $30.00-35.00

All cards $ .50-1.00

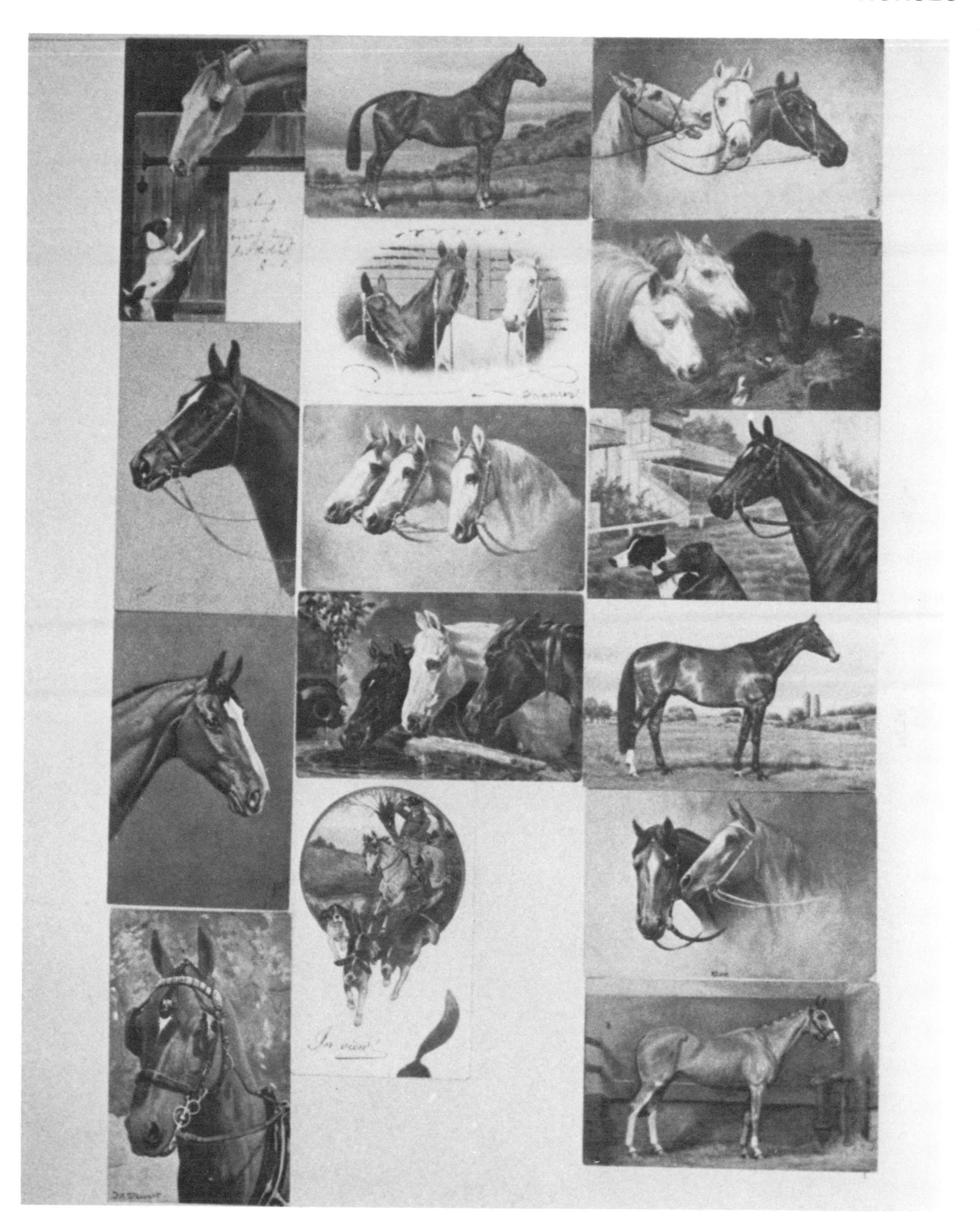

All cards $3.00-4.50

All Cards $3.00-4.00

1. $5.00-6.00	1. $1.00-2.00	1. $3.00-5.00	1. $1.00-2.00
2. $5.00-6.00	2. $1.00-2.00	2. $10.00-12.50	2. $1.00-2.00
3. $5.00-6.00	3. $1.00-2.00	3. $10.00-12.50	3. $3.00-4.00
4. $5.00-6.00	4. $2.00-3.00	4. $10.00-12.50	4. $3.00-5.00
5. $5.00-6.00	5. $2.00-3.00		
6. $5.00-6.00	6. $3.00-4.00		

All cards $1.00-3.00

1. $10.00-12.00
2. $25.00-27.50
3. $12.50-15.00
4. $12.50-15.00

1. $12.50-15.00
2. $20.00-25.00
3. $25.00-27.50
4. $7.00-10.00
5. $7.00-10.00
6. $60.00-80.00

1. $12.50-15.00
2. $12.50-15.00
3. $10.00-12.50
4. $30.00-35.00
5. $15.00-20.00
6. $12.50-15.00

1. $5.00-6.00
2. $4.00-5.00
3. $15.00-17.50
4. $10.00-12.50

1. $80.00-100.00
2. $80.00-100.00
3. $3.00-5.00
4. $3.00-5.00

1. $3.00-5.00
2. $3.00-5.00
3. $5.00-6.00
4. $3.00-5.00

1. $3.00-5.00
2. $3.00-5.00
3. $3.00-5.00
4. $5.00-6.00

1. $3.00-5.00
2. $3.00-4.00
3. $3.00-4.00
4. $3.00-5.00

1. $15.00-20.00
2. $15.00-20.00
3. $15.00-20.00
4. $3.00-5.00

All cards $7.00-8.00

1. $1.00-3.00
2. $1.00-3.00
3. $10.00-12.50
4. $5.00
5. $1.00-3.00
6. $1.00-3.00

1. $7.50-12.50
2. $1.00-3.00
3. $1.00-3.00
4. $5.00
5. $1.00-3.00
6. $1.00-3.00

1. $12.50-15.00
2. $12.50-15.00
3. $12.50-15.00
4. $12.50-15.00
5. $1.00-3.00
6. $1.00-3.00

All cards $5.00-10.00

1. $5.00-6.00
2. $3.00-4.00
3. $4.00-6.00
4. $3.00-4.00
5. $4.00-6.00
6. $4.00-6.00

1. $4.00-6.00
2. $4.00-6.00
3. $3.00-4.00
4. $4.00-6.00

1. $2.00-3.00
2. $4.00-6.00
3. $4.00-6.00
4. $4.00-6.00

1. $4.00-6.00
2. $4.00-6.00
3. $2.00-3.00
4. $3.00-4.00

1. $4.00-6.00
2. $3.00-4.00
3. $3.00-4.00
4. $3.00-4.00

1. $4.00-6.00
2. $4.00-6.00
3. $4.00-5.00
4. $4.00-6.00
5. $4.00-6.00
6. $2.00-3.00

1. $4.00-6.00
2. $4.00-6.00
3. $4.00-6.00
4. $4.00-6.00

1. $3.00-4.00
2. $3.00-4.00
3. $4.00-6.00
4. $4.00-6.00

1. $1.00-2.00
2. $3.00-4.00
3. $3.00-4.00
4. $ .50-1.00

1. $8.00-10.00
2. $12.50-15.00
3. $3.00-5.00
4. $2.00-3.00

1. $10.00-12.50
2. $12.50-17.50
3. $20.00-25.00
4. $15.00-20.00
5. $7.00-10.00
6. $1.00-2.00

1. $3.00-5.00
2. $1.00-2.00
3. $17.50-20.00
4. $3.00-5.00
5. $3.00-5.00
6. $1.00-3.00

1. $2.00-4.00
2. $3.00-4.00
3. $ .50-1.00
4. $ .50-1.00

1. $3.00-4.00
2. $3.00-4.00
3. $1.00-3.00
4. $ .50-1.00

1. $1.00-2.00
2. $1.00-2.00
3. $3.00-4.00
4. $10.00-15.00
5. $6.50-8.00
6. $1.00-2.00

1. $4.00-5.00
2. $5.00-7.00
3. $2.00-3.00
4. $4.00-5.00
5. $4.00-5.00
6. $1.00-2.00

1. $1.00-2.00
2. $ .50- .75
3. $ .50- .75
4. $1.00-2.00
5. $ .50- .75
6. $10.00-12.50

1. $10.00-15.00
2. $ .50-.75
3. $1.00-2.00
4. $2.00-3.00

1. $1.00-2.00
2. $2.00-3.00
3. $2.00-3.00
4. $2.00-3.00

1. $2.00-3.00
2. $ .50-.75
3. $1.00-2.00
4. $5.00-7.00

1. $1.00-2.00
2. $8.00-10.00
3. $2.00-3.00
4. $5.00-6.00
5. $3.00-4.00
6. $7.00-8.00

1. $6.00-7.00
2. $7.00-8.00
3. $9.00-10.00
4. $7.00-8.00

1. $8.00-9.00
2. $7.00-8.00
3. $7.00-8.00
4. $7.00-8.00

1. $1.00-2.00
2. $4.00-5.00
3. $2.00-3.00
4. $6.00-7.00

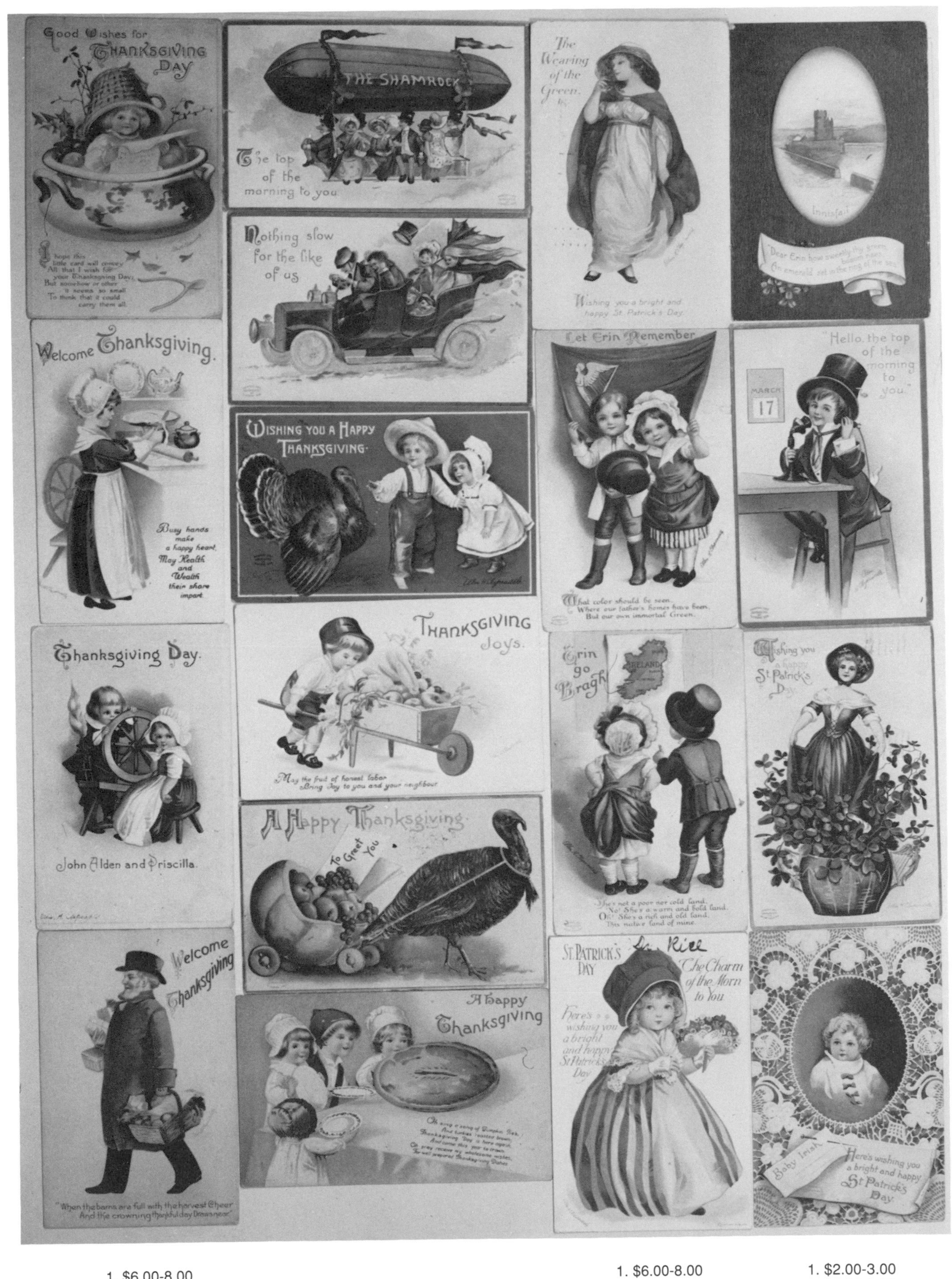

1. $6.00-8.00
2. $7.00-9.00
3. $7.00-9.00
4. $7.00-9.00

1. $5.00-7.00
2. $5.00-7.00
3. $5.00-7.00
4. $6.00-8.00
5. $3.00-5.00
6. $6.00-8.00

1. $6.00-8.00
2. $7.00-9.00
3. $7.00-9.00
4. $6.00-8.00

1. $2.00-3.00
2. $6.00-8.00
3. $6.00-8.00
4. $5.00-7.00

1. $5.00-7.00	1. $7.00-9.00	1. $7.00-8.00	1. $2.00-3.00	1. $2.00-3.00
2. $3.00-4.00	2. $7.00-9.00	2. $7.00-8.00	2. $5.00-7.00	2. $3.00-4.00
3. $7.00-8.00	3. $7.00-9.00	3. $7.00-8.00	3. $2.00-4.00	3. $5.00-7.00
4. $7.00-8.00	4. $7.00-9.00	4. $7.00-8.00	4. $5.00-7.00	4. $6.00-8.00

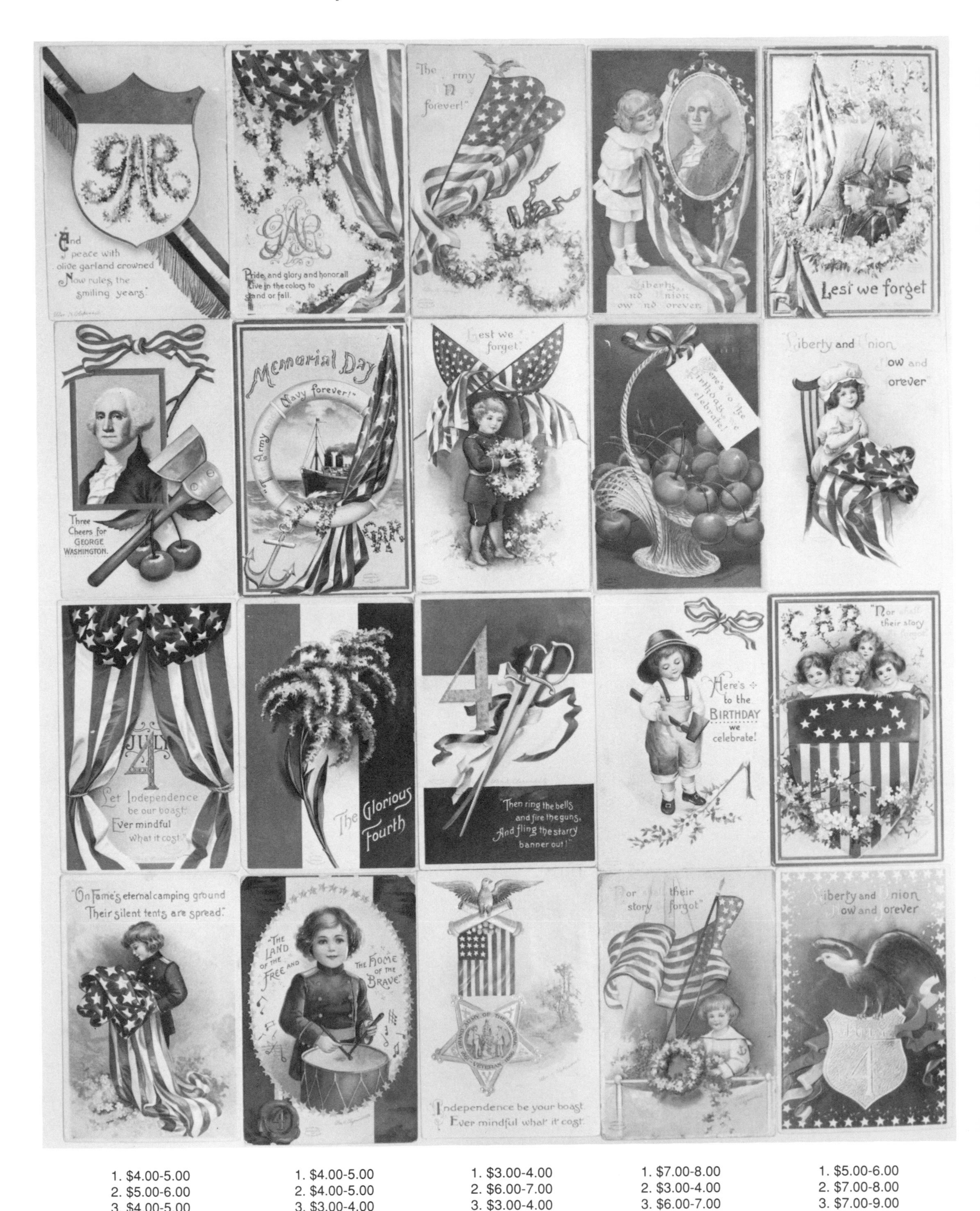

1. $4.00-5.00
2. $5.00-6.00
3. $4.00-5.00
4. $7.00-8.00

1. $4.00-5.00
2. $4.00-5.00
3. $3.00-4.00
4. $7.00-8.00

1. $3.00-4.00
2. $6.00-7.00
3. $3.00-4.00
4. $4.00-5.00

1. $7.00-8.00
2. $3.00-4.00
3. $6.00-7.00
4. $5.00-6.00

1. $5.00-6.00
2. $7.00-8.00
3. $7.00-9.00
4. $3.00-4.00

1. \$8.00-10.00
2. \$8.00-10.00
3. \$2.00-3.00
4. \$5.00-7.00
5. \$2.00-3.00
6. \$2.00-3.00

1. \$7.00-9.00
2. \$8.00-10.00
3. \$5.00-7.00
4. \$2.00-3.00

1. \$7.00-9.00
2. \$6.00-8.00
3. \$2.00-3.00
4. \$8.00-10.00

1. \$7.00-9.00
2. \$7.00-9.00
3. \$5.00-7.00
4. \$7.00-9.00

1. $17.50-22.50
2. $6.00-8.00
3. $6.00-8.00
4. $45.00-60.00*

1. $8.00-10.00
2. $9.00-10.00
3. $8.00-10.00
4. $45.00-60.00*

1. $9.00-10.00
2. $10.00-12.50
3. $9.00-10.00
4. $10.00-12.50

*Mechanical

1. $10.00-12.50
2. $10.00-12.50
3. $10.00-12.50
4. $5.00-6.00

1. $10.00-12.50
2. $8.00-10.00
3. $12.50-15.00
4. $12.50-15.00

1. $6.00-8.00
2. $6.00-8.00
3. $5.00-7.00
4. $6.00-8.00

1. $12.50-15.50
2. $12.50-15.50
3. $7.00-9.00
4. $7.00-9.00
5. $7.00-9.00
6. $6.00-8.00

1. $12.50-15.50
2. $12.50-15.50
3. $12.50-15.50
4. $12.50-15.50
5. $12.50-15.50
6. $12.50-15.50

1. $12.50-15.50
2. $12.50-15.50
3. $12.50-15.50
4. $12.50-15.50

FRANCES BRUNDAGE

1. $6.00-8.00
2. $7.00-9.00
3. $7.00-9.00
4. $8.00-10.00

1. $8.00-10.00
2. $8.00-10.00
3. $8.00-10.00
4. $8.00-10.00

1. $6.00-8.00
2. $6.00-8.00
3. $8.00-10.00
4. $8.00-10.00

1. $7.00-9.00
2. $7.00-9.00
3. $7.00-9.00
4. $7.00-9.00
5. $7.00-9.00
6. $6.00-8.00

All cards $3.00-5.00

All cards $3.00-5.00

All cards $5.00-7.00

All cards $5.00-10.00

All cards $6.00-7.00

H.B. GRIGGS (H.B.G.)

All cards $10.00-13.00

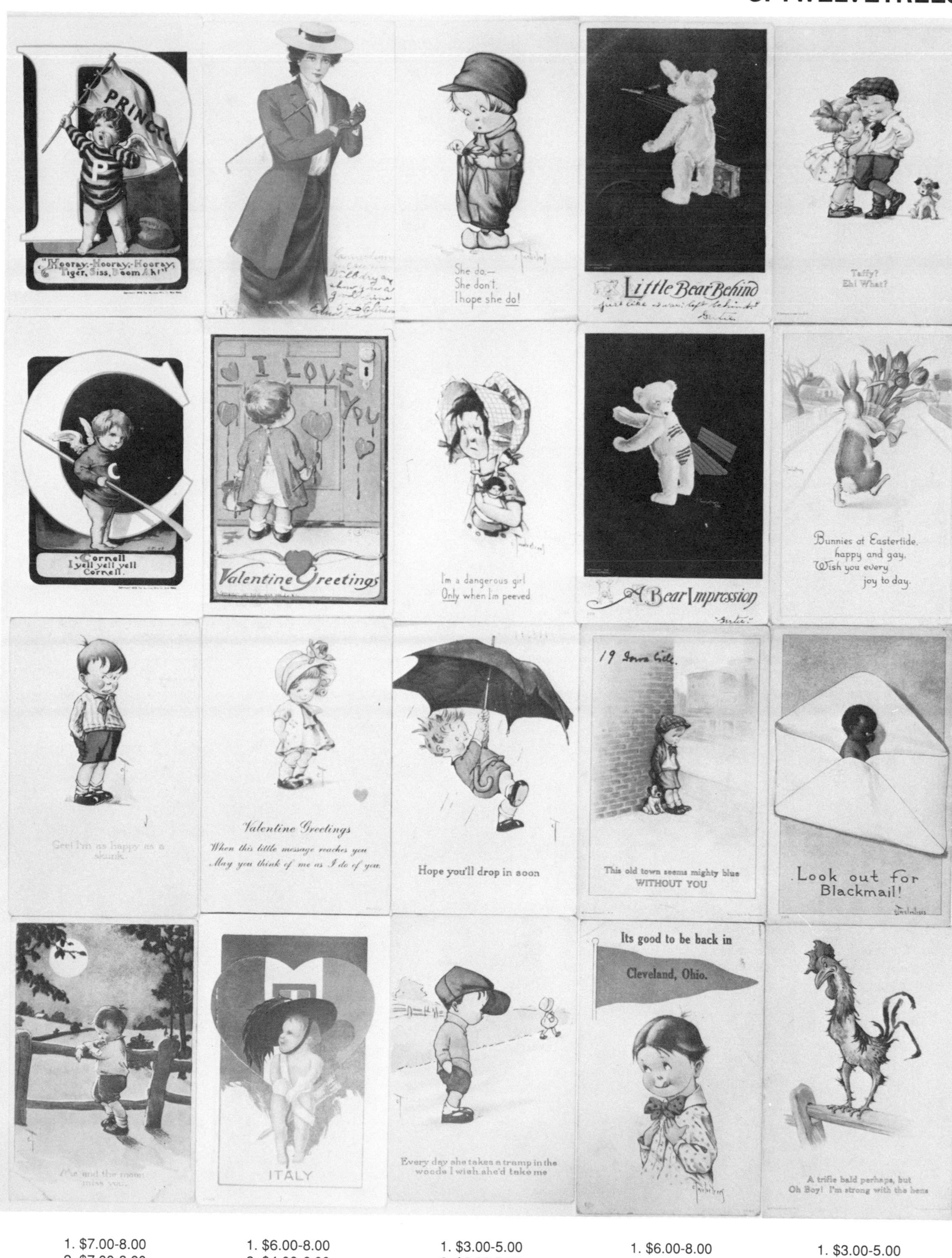

1. $7.00-8.00	1. $6.00-8.00	1. $3.00-5.00	1. $6.00-8.00	1. $3.00-5.00
2. $7.00-8.00	2. $4.00-6.00	2. $3.00-5.00	2. $6.00-8.00	2. $3.00-5.00
3. $3.00-4.00	3. $3.00-5.00	3. $3.00-5.00	3. $3.00-5.00	3. $5.00-7.00
4. $3.00-4.00	4. $6.00-8.00	4. $3.00-5.00	4. $2.00-3.00	4. $3.00-5.00

SPLASHING TIME
Come join me down here at the ocean,
Where breakers are always in motion.
The waves hug the shore—a thing I adore,
You'll find me chuck full of devotion.

YOU'LL BE COPPED
In the name of the law; please stop!
Enough of your dangerous arts.
Cupid, you know, is a vigilant cop
And he'll nab you for stealing hearts.

LOOKING FOR A RAIN-BEAU
When rain is the reigning sensation,
And showers pour down from above;
I yearn for a fellow to bear my umbrella
And share all my torrents of love.

UNDER SHELTER
I'm yearning to have a dear fellow
Join me and share my umbrella;
'twould always be fine, the bright sun would shine,
And Nature be smiling and mellow.

F.S.M.
A SLIPPERY PROPOSITION
Skating is a pleasant pastime
Fills the soul with joy and glee;
You're the only one I'd fall for
Come dear on a skate with me.

I CAN'T GIVE YOU UP
Life at best is but a voyage
On the stormy sea of strife;
Though the boat be rather shaky;—
Give you up? Not on your life.

A STICKER
I'm an expert with poster and paste
And paste up my pictures in haste;
Your picture with art I have stuck on my heart;
And there it will ne'er be defaced.

WHO SAID COLD FEET?
I wish that we could skate together
Until the happy day is done.
Oh, never mind the danger signal;
Where there's no danger, there's no fun.

MAY END IN A TIE
Kissing is a dangerous game
For germs are fostered by it;
But if you will take the blame,
I'll hide my fear and try it.

All cards $4.00

1. $40.00-50.00
2. $25.00-27.50
3. $25.00-27.50

1. $25.00-27.50
2. $25.00-27.50
3. $25.00-27.50
4. $25.00-27.50
5. $25.00-27.50

1. $4.00-5.00
2. $4.00-5.00
3. $4.00-5.00
4. $4.00-5.00
5. $4.00-5.00

KATHERINE GASSAWAY

All cards $5.00-6.00

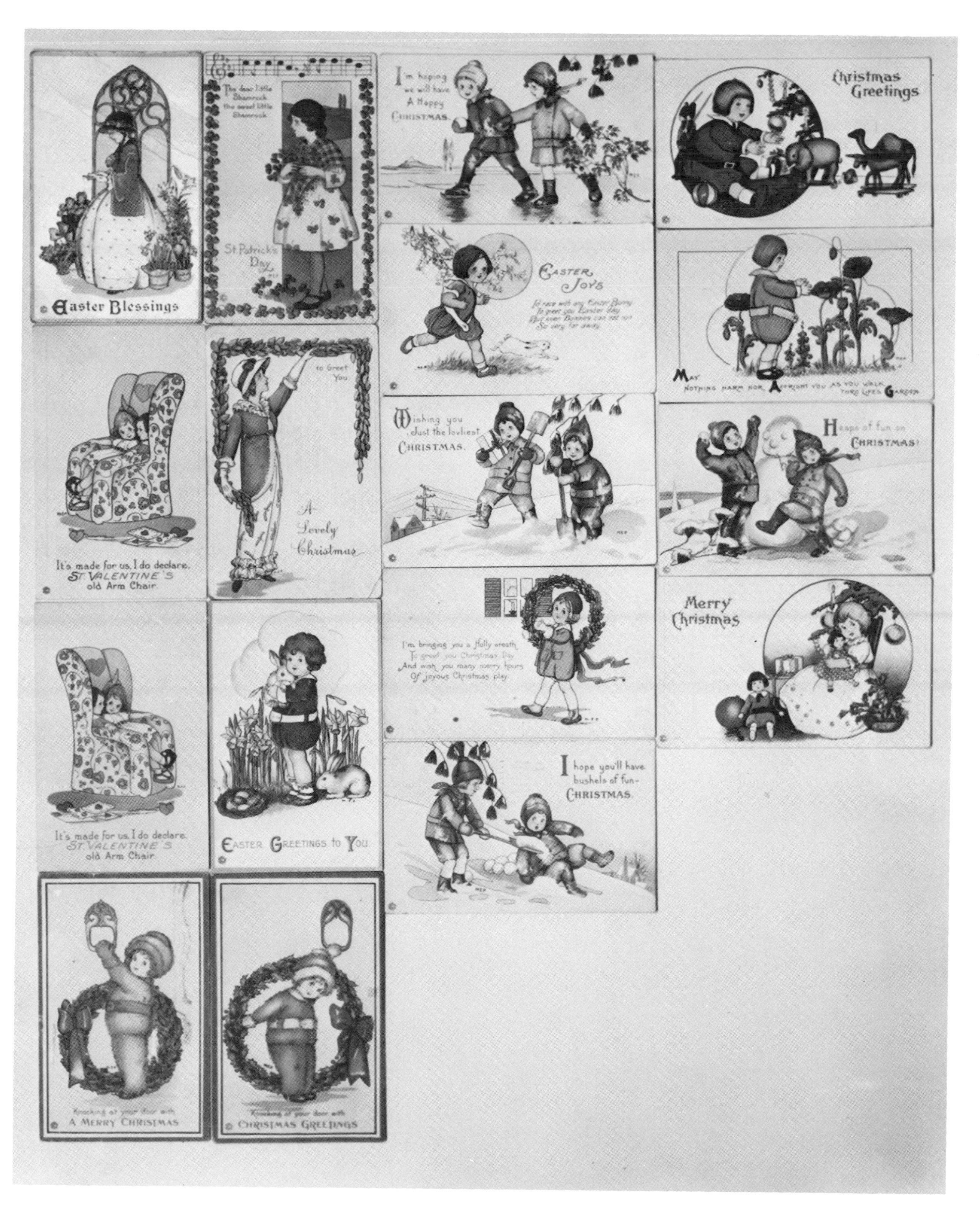

All cards $3.00-4.00

All Embossd in Color

E. CURTIS and GENE CARR

All cards $3.00-5.00

Nos. 1 & 2 are Black and White and by Detroit Publ. Co. Their value is $8.00-10.00 each, all other cards are $10.00-12.50.

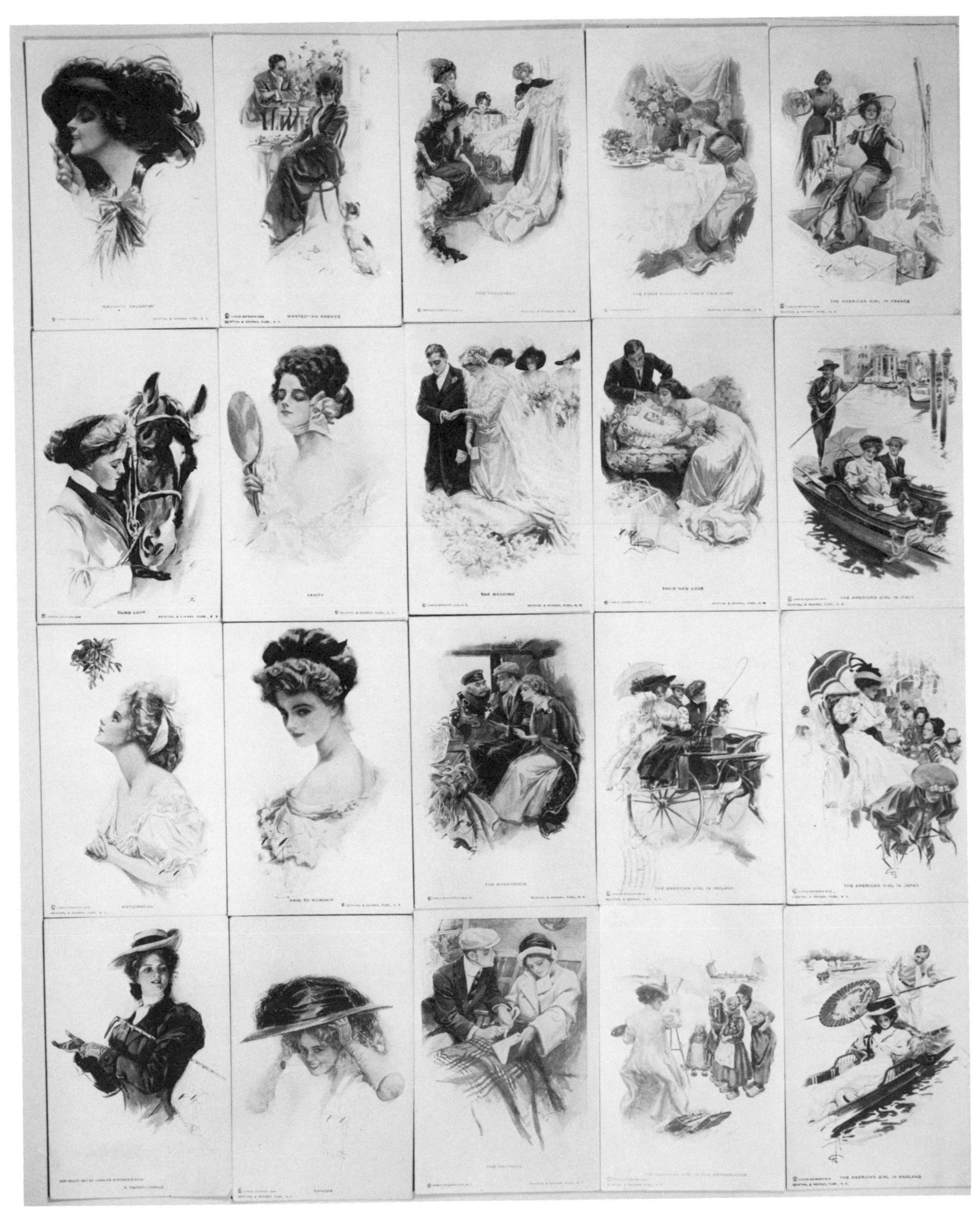

All cards $8.00-12.50

All cards $9.00-12.50

All cards $10.00-15.00

All cards $10.00-15.00

F. EARL CHRISTY

1. $7.00-9.00
2. $7.00-9.00
3. $7.00-9.00
4. $5.00-7.00

1. $5.00-7.00
2. $5.00-7.00
3. $8.00-10.00
4. $8.00-10.00
5. $4.00-6.00
6. $4.00-6.00

1. $5.00-7.00
2. $5.00-7.00
3. $5.00-7.00
4. $5.00-7.00

1. $5.00-7.00
2. $5.00-7.00
3. $5.00-7.00
4. $5.00-7.00

1. $7.00-9.00	1. $7.00-9.00	1. $3.00-5.00	1. $10.00-12.50	1. $12.00-15.00
2. $7.00-9.00	2. $7.00-9.00	2. $3.00-5.00	2. $10.00-12.50	2. $12.00-15.00
3. $5.00-7.00	3. $4.00-6.00	3. $4.00-6.00	3. $10.00-12.50	3. $10.00-12.50
4. $5.00-7.00	4. $4.00-6.00	4. $4.00-6.00	4. $10.00-12.50	4. $10.00-12.50

HOWARD CHANDLER CHRISTY

All cards $4.00-6.00

All cards $2.00-3.00

*Cards signed Tom Yad are the work of Cobb Shinn.

COBB SHINN (COBB X.)

All cards $3.00-5.00

All cards $15.00-17.50

All cards $1.00-3.00

All cards $2.00-4.00 except for April Fool $10.00-15.00 and Halloween $5.00-6.00

All cards $3.00-5.00

All cards $3.00-5.00

All cards $3.00-5.00

1. $8.00-10.00*
2. $2.00-3.00
3. $2.00-3.00
4. $2.00-3.00

*Silk

1. $6.00-8.00
2. $2.00-3.00
3. $2.00-3.00
4. $2.00-3.00

1. $4.00-5.00
2. $8.00-10.00
3. $2.00-3.00
4. $2.00-3.00

1. $4.00-5.00
2. $8.00-10.00
3. $2.00-3.00
4. $2.00-3.00

1. $2.00-3.00
2. $2.00-3.00
3. $2.00-3.00
4. $2.00-3.00

CATHERINE KLEIN (C. KLEIN)

All cards $3.00-5.00

All cards $4.00-6.00

All cards $3.00-5.00

All cards $3.00-5.00

L. H. "DUDE" LARSEN, DOT LARSEN

All cards $ .50-1.00
These cards are Late 1930's & 1940's

All cards $5.00-7.00

L. PETERSON and WINOLD REISS

All cards $6.00-8.00
© By Great Northern Railway (Circa 1930's)

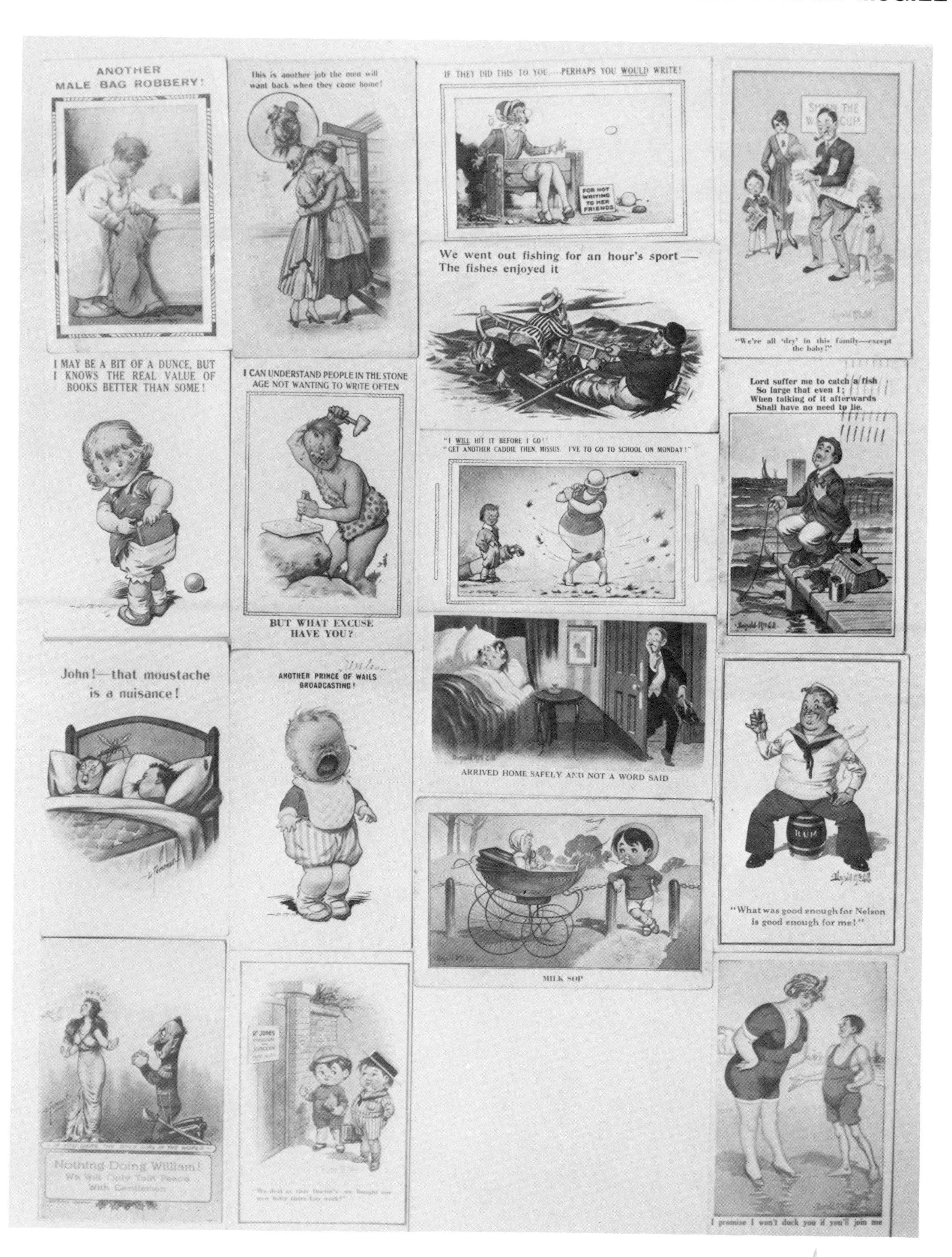

All cards $1.00-2.00

AUGUST HUTAF and R.F. OUTCAULT

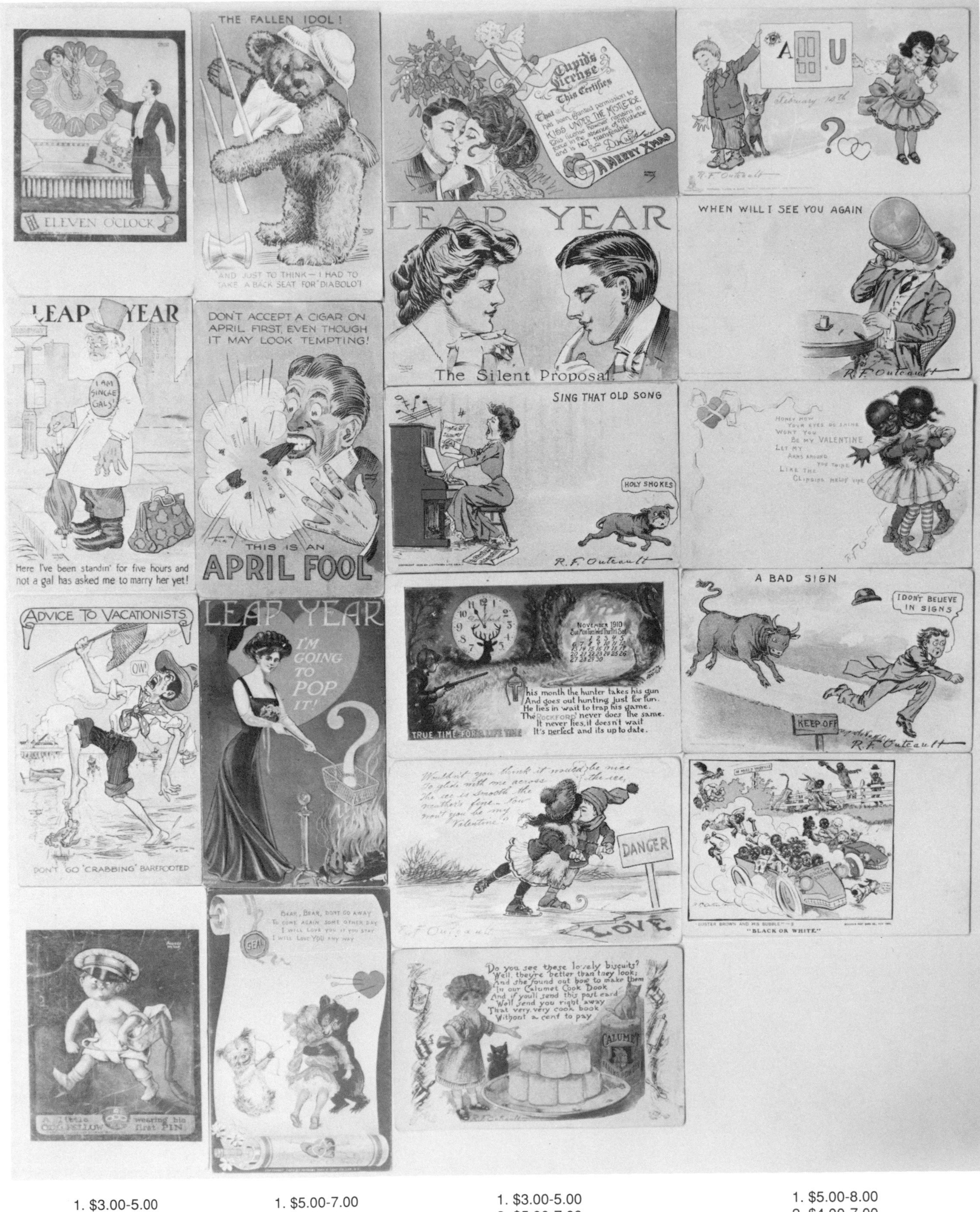

1. $3.00-5.00
2. $3.00-4.00
3. $2.00-4.00
4. $4.00-6.00

1. $5.00-7.00
2. $7.00-9.00
3. $4.00-5.00
4. $5.00-7.00

1. $3.00-5.00
2. $5.00-7.00
3. $4.00-7.00
4. $15.00-20.00
5. $4.00-7.00
6. $15.00-17.00

1. $5.00-8.00
2. $4.00-7.00
3. $5.00-8.00
4. $4.00-7.00
5. $15.00-17.50

All cards $2.00-4.00

CARMICHAEL and WALTER WELLMAN

Wellman Cards $1.00-2.00

All other cards $2.00-4.00

All cards $2.00-4.00

SHERIE, ZULA KENYON, FRANK CAROLYN O' NEILL, W. BRAUN

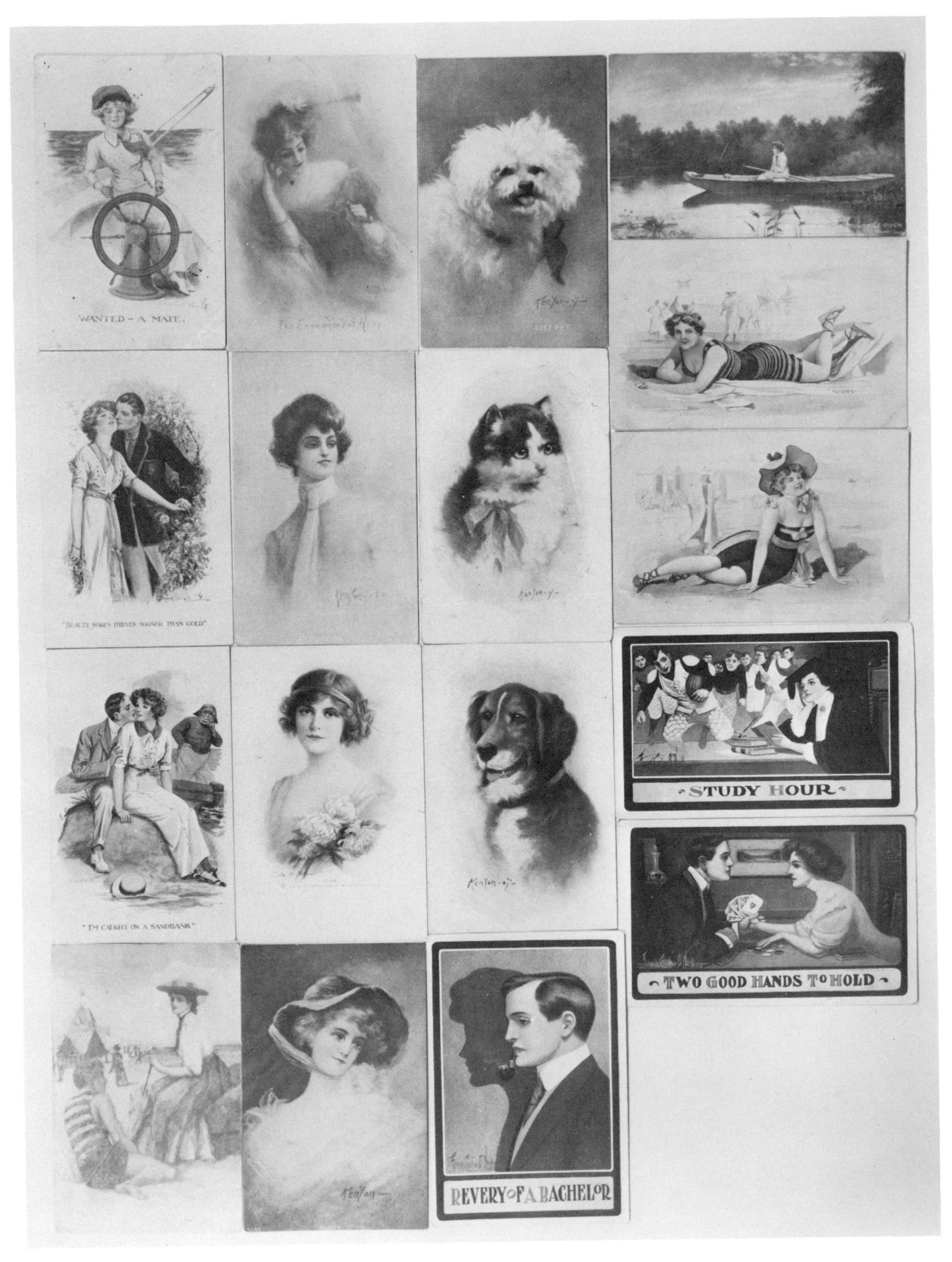

All cards $2.00-4.00

All cards $2.00-4.00

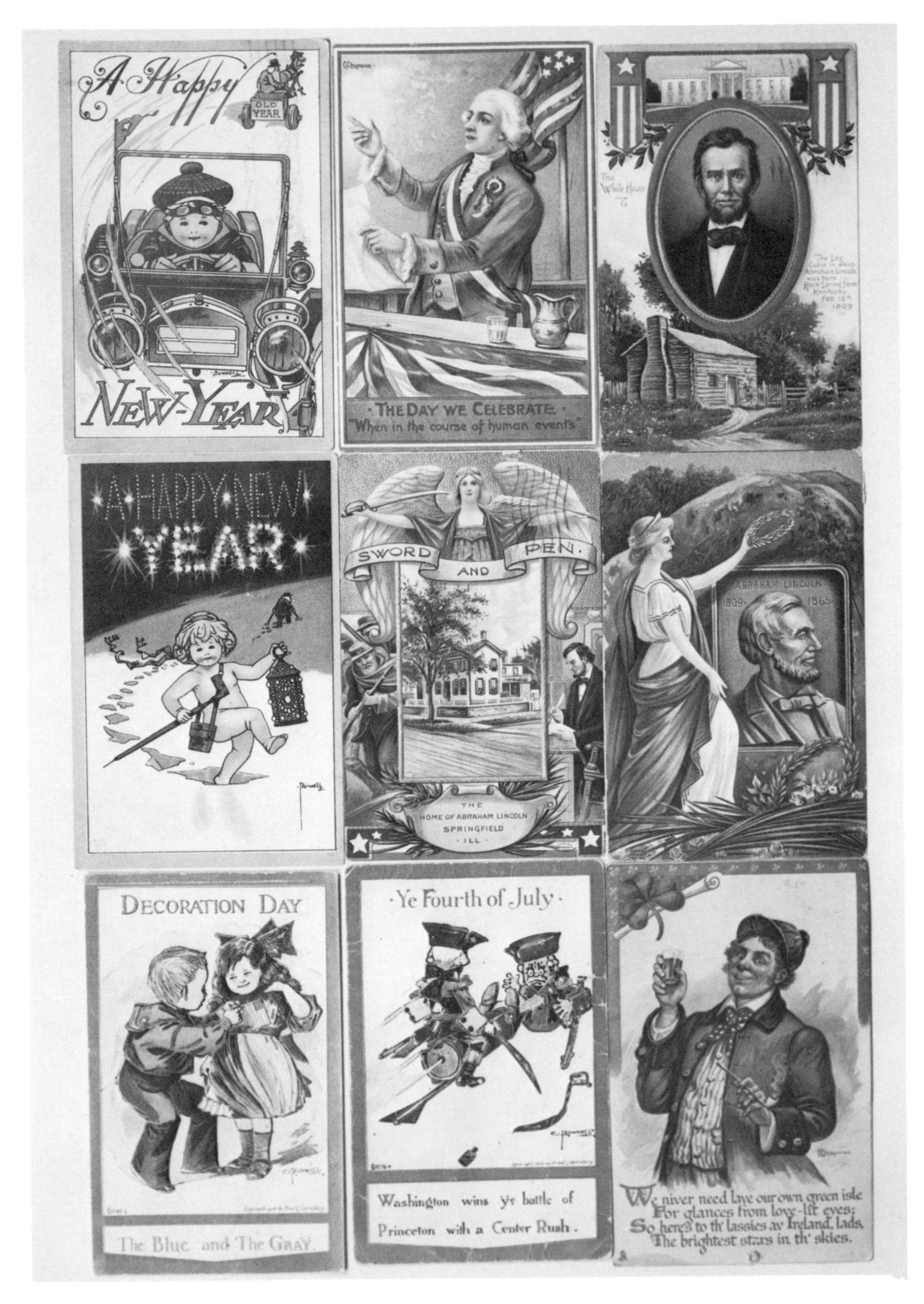

All cards $5.00-7.00

All cards $4.00-6.00

MAY L. FARINI, EDW. G. WASKOW and GOTTARO

All cards $2.00-4.00

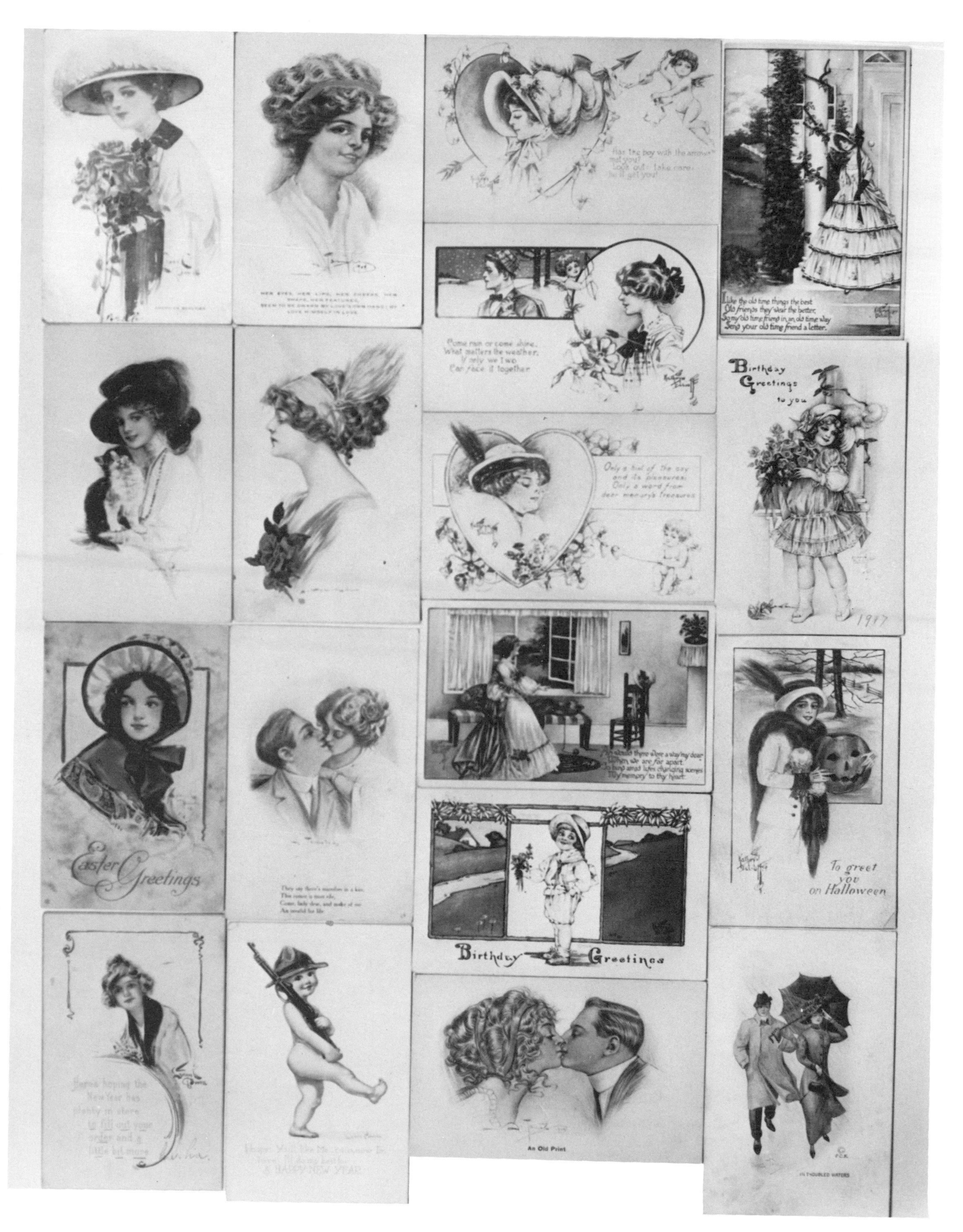

All cards $2.00-4.00

M.L. BLUMENTHAL, FRED SPURGIN, E.R. TYRELL

All cards $2.00-4.00

ALICE LUELLA FIDLER, PEARL EUGENIA FIDLER (LEMUNYON), JAMES MONTGOMERY FLAGG, ANTOINETTE CLARK

All cards $3.00-5.00

Gollings
Chas Graig
J.F. (Tuck)
J.F. (Tuck)

Gollings
Gollings
Gollings
Gollings

F.W. Schultz
F.W. Schultz
R.A. Davenport
R.A. Davenport
Gollings

All cards $4.00-6.00

M.L.A.F.R.
M.L.A.F.R.
M.L.A.F.R.
John Up Yongh

C.A. Voight
V.C. Anderson
Mabel Lucie Atwell
Mabel Lucie Atwell

Ethel Dewees
Ethel Dewees
E.H.D. (Ethel Dewees)
E.H.D. (Ethel Dewees)

E.H.D. (Ethel Dewees)
E.H.D. (Ethel Dewees)
E.H.D. (Ethel Dewees)
E.H.D. (Ethel Dewees)
E.H.D. (Ethel Dewees)
Mabel Lucie Atwell

All cards $2.50-4.00

L.G. Humphries
O. Gross
P Ebner

C.B.
F.Y. Cory
P. Ebner
P. Ebner

F.E. Nosworthy
H.F. Lehman
DeGarmes
DeGarmes

All cards $3.00-5.00

R.T.	Ruth Welch Surr	Ruth Welch Surr	Jessie Wilcox Smith
R.T.	Ruth Welch Surr	Ruth Welch Surr	Jessie Wilcox Smith
C.B.T.	Mary Sigsbeeker	Mary Sigsbeeker	Jessie Wilcox Smith
C.B.T.	Mary Sigsbeeker	Mary Sigsbeeker	Jennie Nystrom
		Jennie Nystrom	
		Jennie Nystrom	

All cards $3.00-5.00

OTHER ARTISTS – CHILDREN

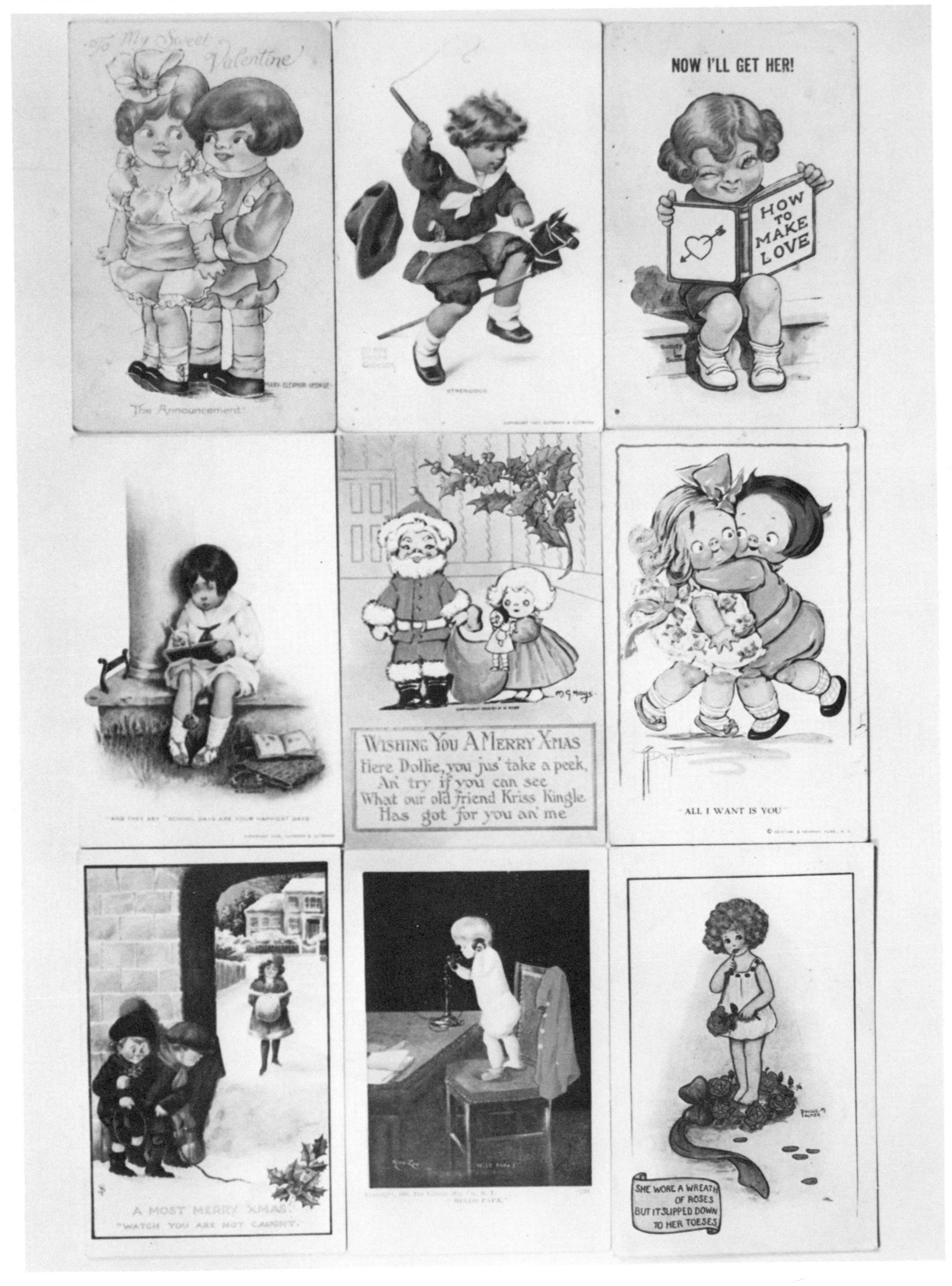

Mary Eleanor George	$3.00-4.00	Bessie Pease Gutmann	$4.00-5.00	Dudley Buxton	$1.00-2.00
M. Grimball	$2.00-3.00	M.G. Hays	$7.50-10.00	G. Drayton	$12.50-15.00
S.F (Monogram)	$2.00-3.00	Alice Lee	$2.00-3.00	Phyliss M. Palmer	$2.00-3.00

Pillard	$5.00-6.00	Robt. Robinson	$6.00-7.00	Raphael Kirchner	$30.00-35.00	Robt. Robinson	$5.00-6.00
Grace Wiederseim	$12.50-15.00	John T. McCutcheon	$5.00-6.00	Raphael Kirchner	$30.00-35.00	Robt. Robinson	$5.00-6.00
Grace Wiederseim	$12.50-15.00	John T. McCutcheon	$5.00-6.00	M.M. Grimball	$3.00-4.00	Robt. Robinson	$5.00-6.00

Bottom Left – Back side of John T. McCutcheon card

Bottom right – Wiederseim $12.50-15.00

E.B. Kemble	P. Crosby	D.P. Crane	D.P. Crane
E.B. Kemble	P. Crosby	D.P. Crane	H.H.
E.B. Kemble	Bishop	P. Crosby	H.H.
Arthur Gill	Arthur Gill	H.H.	H.H.
		Bishop	
		Bishop	

All cards $2.00-4.00

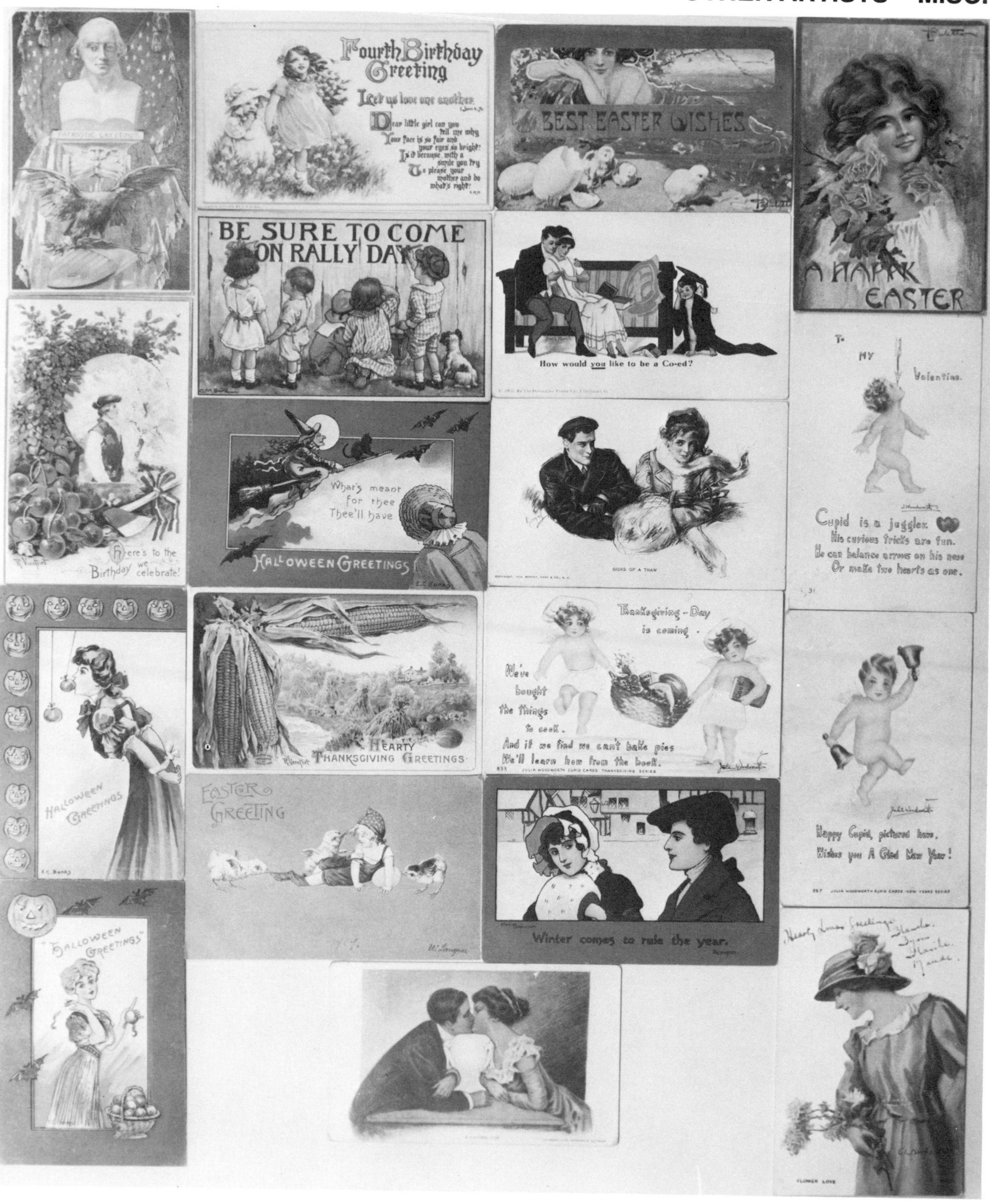

R. Veentliet	$2.00-4.00
R. Veentliet	$2.00-4.00
E.C. Banks	$2.00-4.00
E.C. Banks	$4.00-8.00
E.C. Banks	$7.00-8.00

C.M. Burd	$2.00-4.00
C.M. Burd	$2.00-4.00
E.C. Banks	$7.00-8.00
R. Veentliet	$2.00-4.00
W. Langmer	$2.00-4.00

T. Bieletto	$2.00-4.00
Frank Murch	$2.00-4.00
Williams	$2.00-4.00
Julia Woodworth	$2.00-4.00
Ethel Parkinson	$2.00-4.00

T. Bieletto	$2.00-4.00
Julia Woodworth	$2.00-4.00
Julia Woodworth	$2.00-4.00
C.W. Barbor	$2.00-4.00

Bottom center
M.M. Grimball $2.00-4.00

OTHER ARTISTS – MISC.

Chas A. McClellan	$2.00-4.00
W. Darling	$2.00-4.00
Anthony Guarino	$2.00-4.00
Anthony Guarino	$2.00-4.00

Anthony Guarino	$2.00-4.00
Anthony Guarino	$2.00-4.00
Anthony Guarino	$2.00-4.00
Anthony Guarino	$2.00-4.00

B.	$1.00-1.50
Mary Golay	$2.00-4.00
Mary Golay	$2.00-4.00
B.	$1.00-1.50
N. Drummond	$2.00-4.00

Norman Rockwell	$30.00-40.00
Mary Golay	$2.00-4.00

C. Allen Gilbert
C. Allen Gilbert
C. Allen Gilbert
C. Allen Gilbert

St. John
M. Dulk
M. Dulk
C. Allen Gilbert

St. John
St. John
St. John
St. John

H. King
H. King
H. King
H. King

H. King
H. King
H. King
H. King

All cards $4.00-6.00

OTHER ARTISTS – MISC.

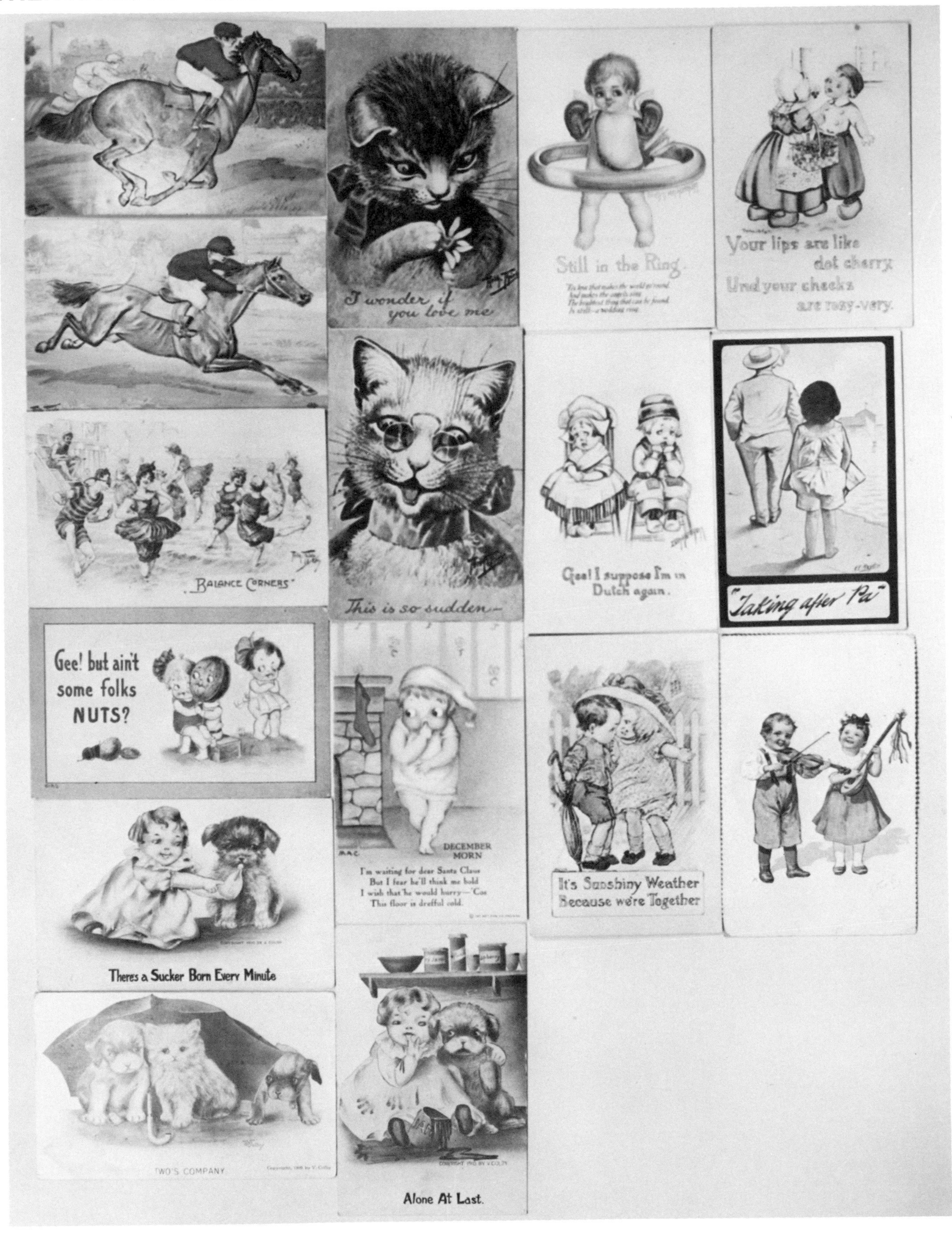

Arthur Thiele $10.00-12.00
Arthur Thiele $10.00-12.00
Arthur Thiele $5.00-6.00
E. Von Hartmann $1.00-2.00
V. Colby $1.00-2.00
V. Colby $1.00-2.00

Arthur Thiele $10.00-12.00
Arthur Thiele $10.00-12.00
M.A.C. $4.00-5.00
V. Colby $1.00-2.00

Evelyn Von Hartmann $2.00-4.00
Evelyn Von Hartmann $2.00-4.00
W.H.L. $2.00-4.00

Dennison $ .50-1.00
A.E. Hayden $ .50-1.00
K Fiertag $1.00-1.50

Arthur Butcher
Myer
Myer
Sadie Wendell Mitchell

J.V. McFall
J.V. McFall
J.V. McFall
Sadie Wendell Mitchell

Marion Miller
Marion Miller
Lou Mayer
Loy Mayer
Lou Mayer
Sadie Wendell Mitchell

Marion Miller
Marion Miller
Marion Miller
Loy Mayer

All cards $2.00-4.00

OTHER ARTISTS – MISC.

R. Ford Harbor
H.N. Dihlen
Frances Day
F.D. Foster

A. Heinze
A. Heinze
L. Kish
Jon Marcos

J. Knowles Hare, Jr.
J. Knowles Hare, Jr.
J. Knowles Hare, Jr.
J. Knowles Hare, Jr.

M. Marco
The Kinneys
Leon Moran
J. Knowles Hare, Jr.

All cards $3.00-5.00

Bella Gross	$2.00-4.00	Fred S. Manning	$2.00-4.00	A. Asti	$5.00-6.00	A. Asti	$5.00-6.00
Bella Gross	$2.00-4.00	Frederick Greene	$2.00-4.00	Jay Francis Brown	$2.00-4.00	A. Asti	$5.00-6.00
Marion Reed	$2.00-4.00	Lillian Woolsey Hunter	$2.00-4.00	Lillian Woolsey Hunter	$2.00-4.00	A. Asti	$5.00-6.00
Mary Horsefall	$2.00-4.00	Harrison	$2.00-4.00	Harrison	$2.00-4.00	A. Asti	$5.00-6.00

OTHER ARTISTS – MISC.

H. Harmony $9.00-11.00*
G. Reiter Brill $2.00-3.00
G. Reiter Brill $2.00-3.00
H. LaPraik Ball $1.00-2.00

M. Greiner $3.00-5.00
C. Gibson $7.00-10.00
C. Gibson $7.00-10.00
H. LaPraik Ball $2.00-4.00

G. Howard Hilder $5.00-7.00
G. Howard Hilder $5.00-7.00
J. Jones $4.00-6.00
W. Haskell Coffin $5.00-7.00

G. Howard Hilder $3.00-5.00
G. Howard Hilder $5.00-7.00
G. Howard Hilder $5.00-7.00
G. Howard Hilder $5.00-7.00

*Mechanical

All cards $1.50-3.00

All cards $1.00-2.00 except Negro with watermelon $5.00-7.00

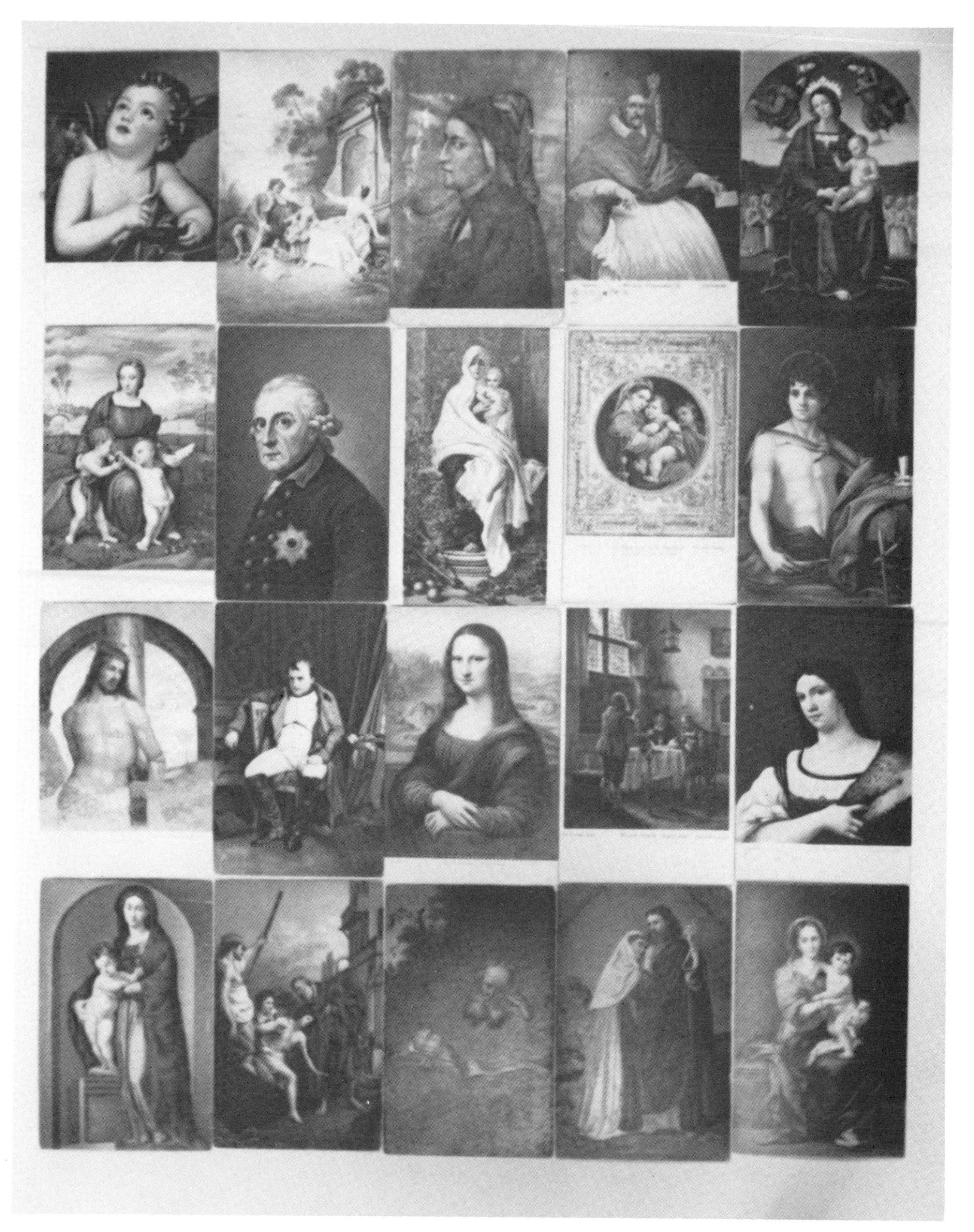

All cards $1.00-2.00

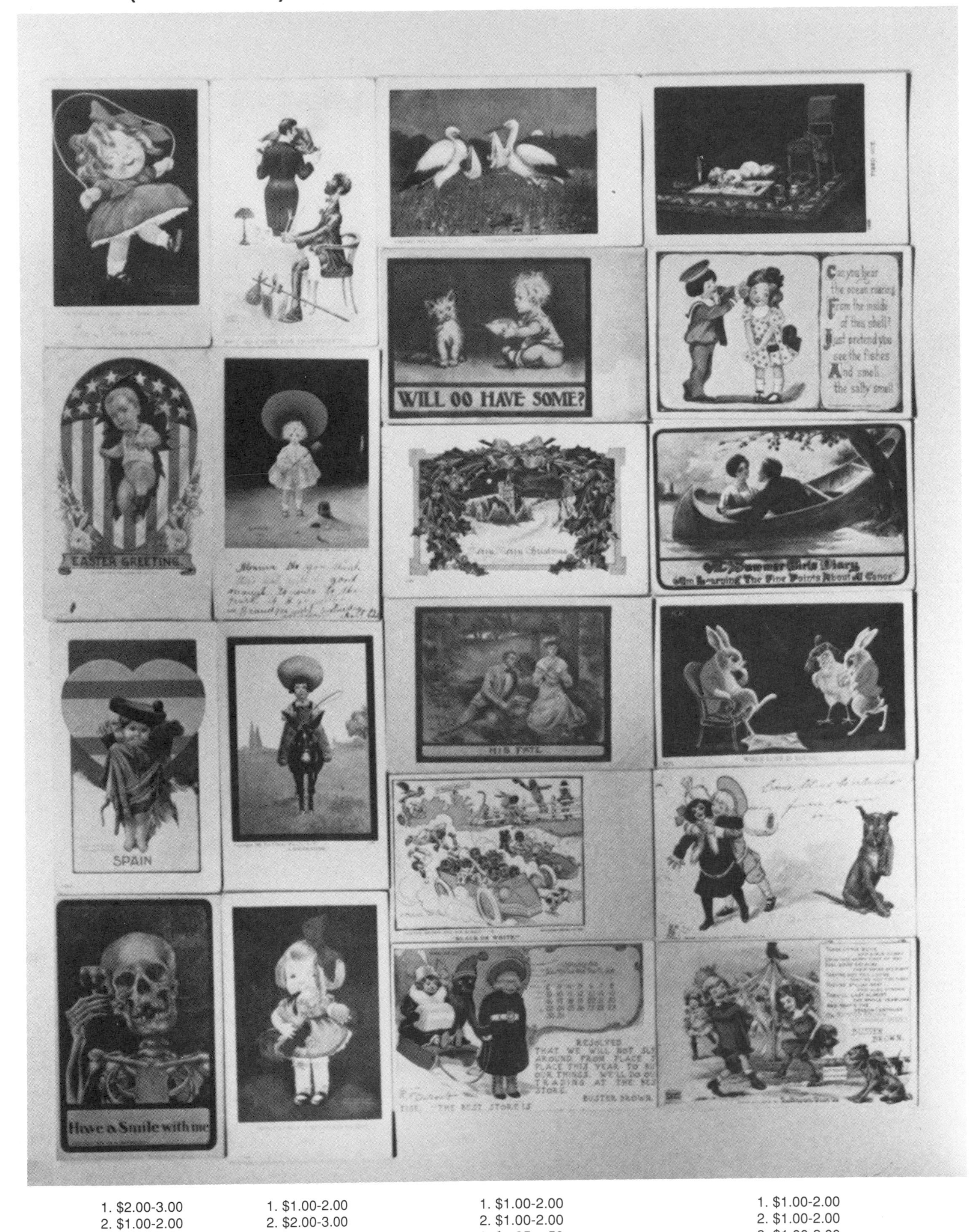

1. $2.00-3.00
2. $1.00-2.00
3. $3.00-4.00
4. $1.00-2.00

1. $1.00-2.00
2. $2.00-3.00
3. $2.00-3.00
4. $2.00-3.00

1. $1.00-2.00
2. $1.00-2.00
3. $ .25- .50
4. $1.00-2.00
5. $10.00-12.00
6. $10.00-12.50

1. $1.00-2.00
2. $1.00-2.00
3. $1.00-2.00
4. $1.00-2.00
5. $6.00-8.00
6. $10.00-12.50

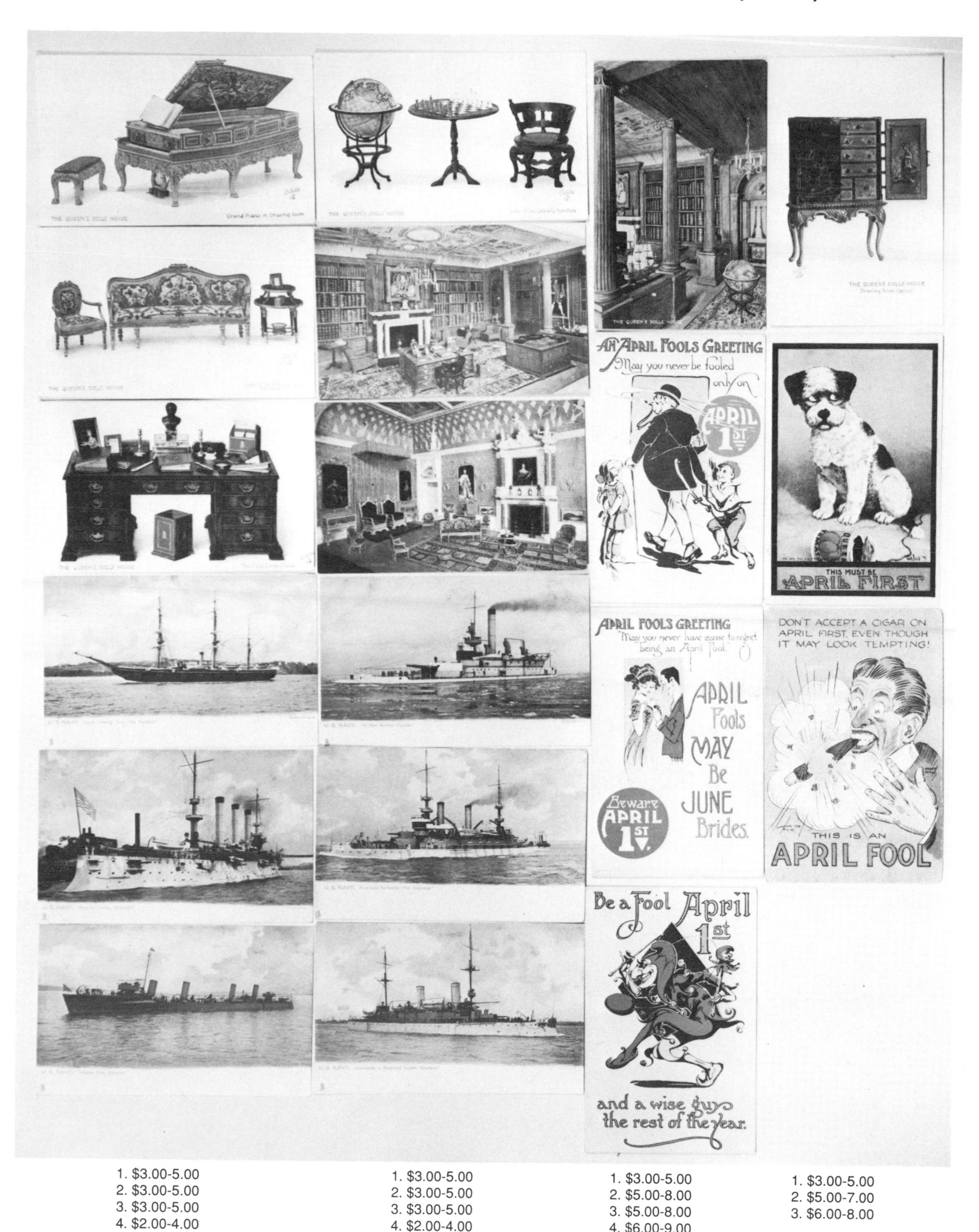

1. $3.00-5.00
2. $3.00-5.00
3. $3.00-5.00
4. $2.00-4.00
5. $2.00-4.00
6. $2.00-4.00

1. $3.00-5.00
2. $3.00-5.00
3. $3.00-5.00
4. $2.00-4.00
5. $2.00-4.00
6. $2.00-4.00

1. $3.00-5.00
2. $5.00-8.00
3. $5.00-8.00
4. $6.00-9.00

1. $3.00-5.00
2. $5.00-7.00
3. $6.00-8.00

TUCK (PUBLISHER) INDEPENDENCE DAY and EDUCATIONAL SERIES

1. $5.00-6.50
2. $5.00-6.50
3. $5.00-6.50
4. $5.00-6.50
5. $15.00-20.00
6. $ .50-1.00

1. $5.00-6.50
2. $5.00-6.50
3. $5.00-6.50
4. $5.00-6.50
5. $15.00-20.00
6. $ .50-1.00

1. $5.00-6.50
2. $5.00-6.50
3. $5.00-6.50
4. $5.00-6.50
5. $15.00-20.00
6. $10.00-15.00

All cards $2.00-3.00

1. $2.00-3.00
2. $2.00-3.00
3. $4.00-5.00
4. $2.00-3.00

1. $3.00-4.00
2. $ .50-1.00
3. $ .50-1.00
4. $1.00-2.00
5. $7.00-10.00
6. $2.00-3.00

1. $2.00-4.00
2. $2.00-4.00
3. $2.00-4.00
4. $2.00-4.00

1. $ .50-1.00
2. $3.00-4.00
3. $3.00-5.00
4. $1.00-2.00
5. $7.00-10.00
6. $1.00-3.00

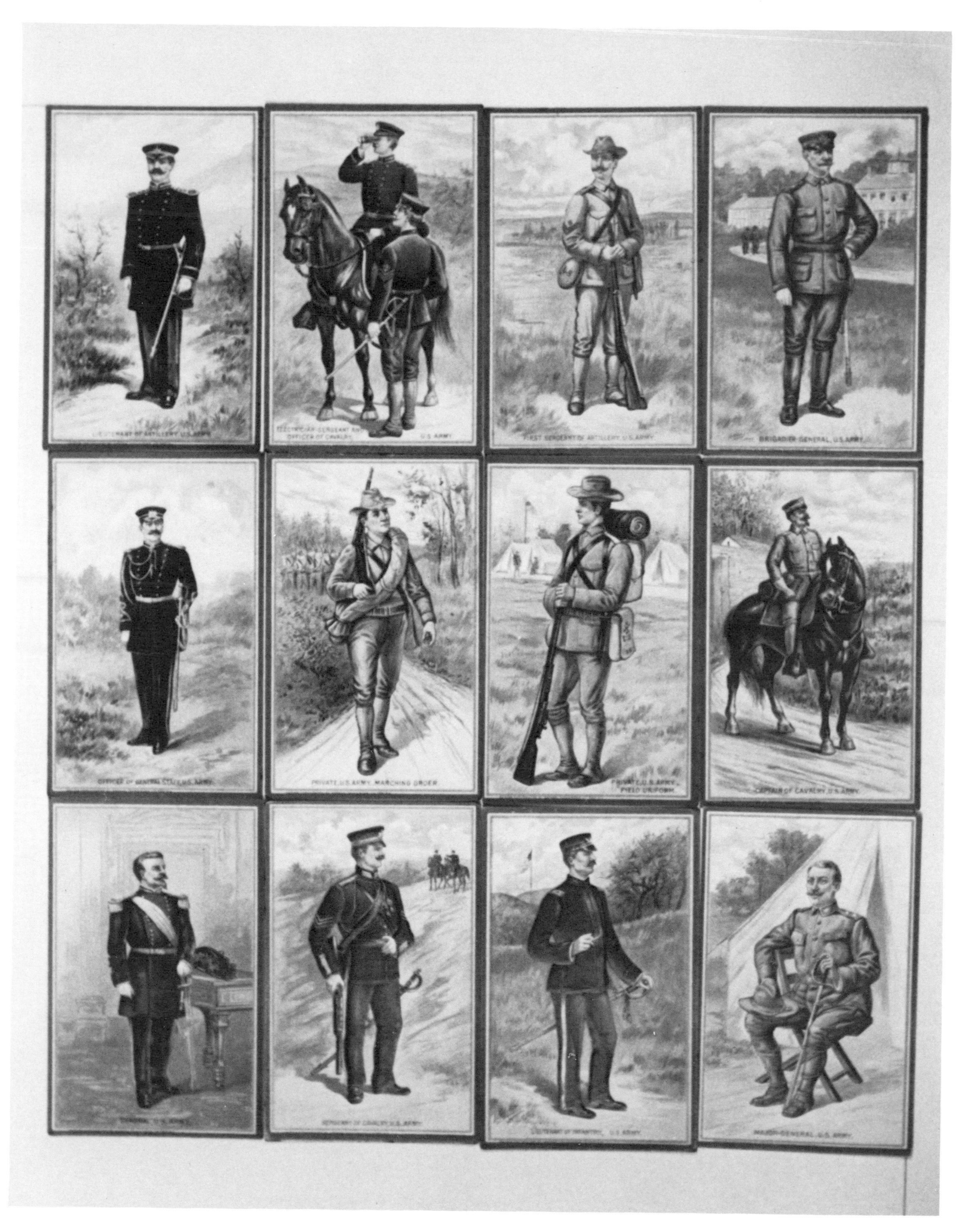

All cards $10.00-12.00

1. $ .50-1.00
2. $ .50-1.00
3. $ .50-1.00
4. $ .50-1.00

1. $7.00-9.00
2. $10.00-12.50
3. $10.00-12.50
4. $ .50-1.00

1. $7.00-9.00
2. $10.00-12.50
3. $10.00-12.50
4. $ .50-1.00

1. $4.00-5.00
2. $1.00-2.00
3. $4.00-5.00
4. $ .50-1.00

1. $ .50-1.00
2. $ .50-1.00
3. $2.00-3.00
4. $1.00-2.00

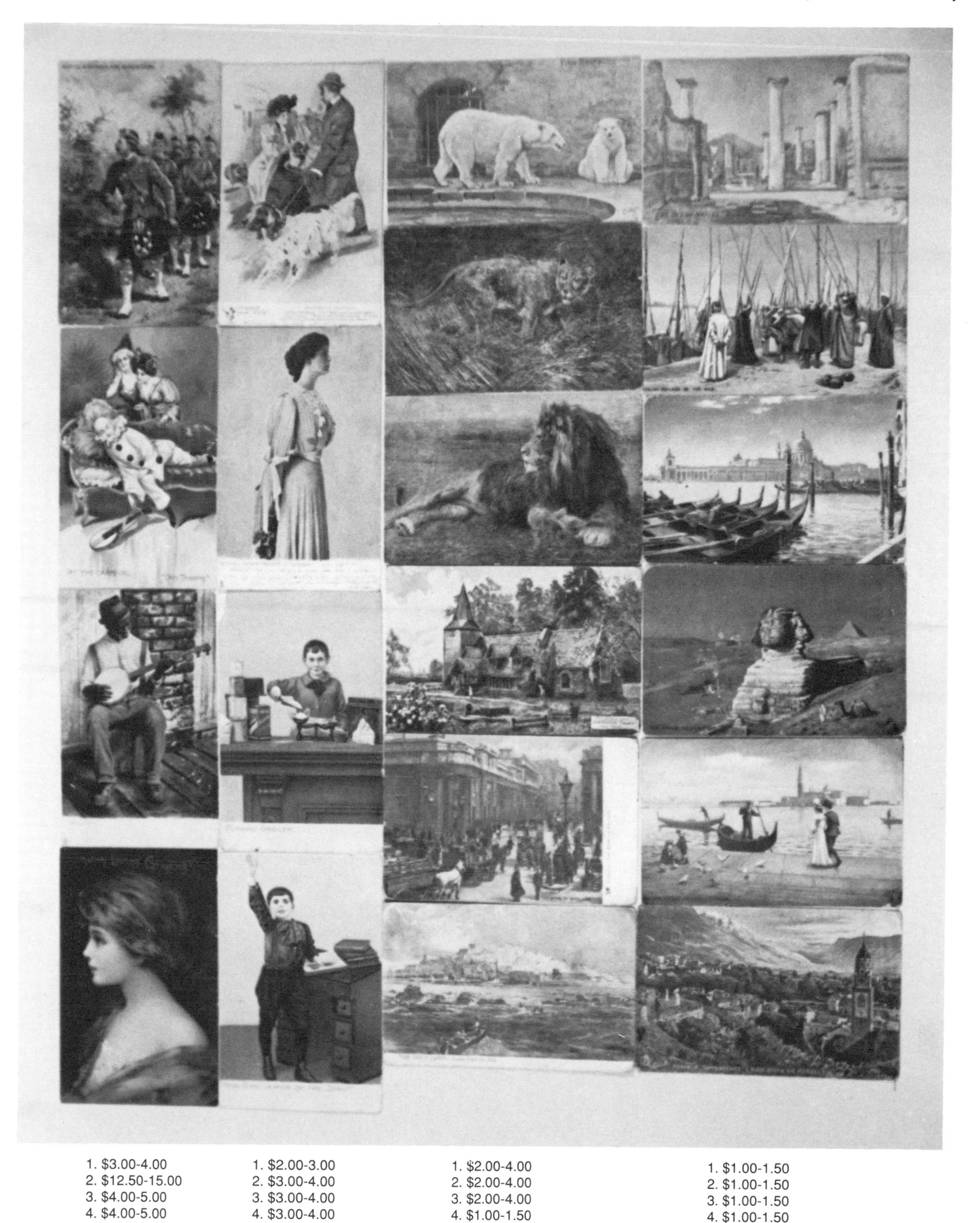

1. $3.00-4.00
2. $12.50-15.00
3. $4.00-5.00
4. $4.00-5.00

1. $2.00-3.00
2. $3.00-4.00
3. $3.00-4.00
4. $3.00-4.00

1. $2.00-4.00
2. $2.00-4.00
3. $2.00-4.00
4. $1.00-1.50
5. $ .50-1.00
6. $1.00-1.50

1. $1.00-1.50
2. $1.00-1.50
3. $1.00-1.50
4. $1.00-1.50
5. $1.00-1.50
6. $1.00-1.50

All cards $ .50-1.00

INDEX

Note: Due to the many cards in this book, I did not index every single card. Most of the highly collectible cards *are* indexed. Artist index is separate.

DIRECTORY OF ARTISTS

K

L

M

N

O

P

R

S

T

U

V

W

XYZ